"This is a powerful book that finally dispels the myth that defending oneself is 'unchristian.' As believers we are duty bound to teach our children that honor, justice, courage in the face of adversity, and defending the weak are not only the right things to own and do, they are a Christian's obligation. Bravo! Paul Coughlin, for giving back to us our warrior spirit."

—**Brad Stine**
Comedian, author, actor

Books by
# Paul Coughlin
FROM BETHANY HOUSE PUBLISHERS

---

*Married . . . But Not Engaged*

*No More Christian Nice Guy*

*No More Christian Nice Guy Study Guide*

# PAUL COUGHLIN

# NO MORE JELLYFISH, CHICKENS, OR WIMPS

BETHANYHOUSE
MINNEAPOLIS, MINNESOTA

Published by Bethany House Publishers
11400 Hampshire Avenue South
Bloomington, Minnesota 55438

Bethany House Publishers is a division of
Baker Publishing Group, Grand Rapids, Michigan.

Printed in the United States of America

ISBN-13:  978-0-7642-0242-1
ISBN-10:  0-7642-0242-1

**Library of Congress Cataloging-in-Publication Data**

Coughlin, Paul T.
    No more jellyfish, chickens, or wimps: raising secure, assertive kids in a tough world / Paul Coughlin.
        Summary: "Paul Coughlin gives parents good news: that they can nurture assertive—not aggressive or passive—children able to live abundantly and love God and their neighbor as they love themselves. He shows parents how to instill virtues of toughness, wisdom, and courage in their children rather than fake 'niceness.' "— Provided by publisher.
        Includes bibliographical references.
        ISBN-13:  978-0-7642-0242-1 (hardcover ; alk. paper)
        ISBN-10:  0-7642-0242-1 (hardcover ; alk. paper)
        1. Parenting—Psychological aspects.  2. Self-esteem.  3. Assertiveness training.
    I. Title.
        HQ755.8.C677      2007
        649'.1—dc22                                                    2007007106

# ABOUT THE AUTHOR

PAUL COUGHLIN, author of *No More Christian Nice Guy,* and coauthor of *Married . . . But Not Engaged,* hosts a radio talk show on The Dove in southern Oregon, and speaks internationally about childhood difficulties that lead toward passive living. Paul is a founding member of GodMen and has been interviewed by the *New York Times, Newsweek, LA Times,* C-SPAN, *Focus on the Family, Good Morning America, Nightline,* and numerous radio and television stations. His articles have appeared in *New Man, Faithworks, Today's Christian Woman,* along with other periodicals, and he is a contributing writer and official blogger for Crosswalk.com. A former Christian Nice Guy, Paul is a passionate husband to Sandy, enthusiastic father to three active children, and veteran youth soccer coach. The Coughlins live in Oregon.

# ACKNOWLEDGMENTS

Thank you to the following who gave their insight, guidance, and practical help to make this work and mission possible:

Barbara Wiedenbeck, Dennis Hughett Jr., Janet Grant, Dr. Laura, Timothy Arthur, Jason Ehrlich, Ted Darnall, Mike Smith, Brian Doyle, Michael Levine, John Renken, Mark Galli, Glenn Sacks, Brad Wilcox, Perry Atkinson, Senator Jason Atkinson, Bill Strock, Jeff Smith, Bill Gallagher, and Peter Grant.

The team at Bethany House: Christopher Soderstrom, Kyle Duncan, Julie Smith, Tim Peterson, Linda White, Jim Hart, Brett Benson.

Also, thank you to all the children whom I have had the pleasure to coach, especially the St. Mary's Varsity Soccer Team, Division Champions 2006.

The men of GodMen: Mike, Brad, Ken, Dave, Michael, and more to come. And to all of those who were bullied and thought no one heard you, no one cared.

And, of course, our children, who help comprise this mini-nation called the Coughlin family.

# CONTENTS

# TIMID LIVING: THE ESSENCE OF THE PROBLEM

*"My marriage is disintegrating, and my wife doesn't respect me. She says I drain her of energy. Is it too late?"*

*"My husband is a nice man, but he's not a good man. Our home is falling apart."*

*"My son keeps letting his friends walk all over him. Can you help him?"*

*"My daughter was a victim of cyber-bullying. She doesn't want to go to school anymore."*

*"I don't push back at work, and it ends up hurting me and my family. But I'm not supposed to push back . . . right?"*

*"My mother-in-law steamrolls me and then compliments me on behaving like a 'nice Christian woman.' I'm furious, but I don't know what to do about it."*

*"When I was young, Mom and Dad said to turn my cheek to all the bullying from the other kids. I can't stand what my schoolmates did to me. I'm so angry that I let it happen, but nothing has changed—I keep letting similar things happen to me now."*

*"When will I feel strong, like a man?"*

Why begin a book about parenting with adult problems and adult complaints? Because for many their struggle with being timid and passive began during their childhood. They were told as children that nice boys and girls, especially Christian kids, don't exert their will, don't stand up and fight, and don't do conflict. Their lives today are in various states of disarray and even ruin because of what they were taught (both intentionally and unintentionally). They're soft, compliant, and pleasant instead of assertive, courageous, and virtuous.

Many of these adults, the ones making these statements and asking these questions, are just beginning to see how cautious living—solidified during their upbringing and fortified by messages they continue to receive—is holding them back. They've been stunted in marriage, in career, in child-raising; they've been stifled in their ability to understand God's character and receive His love.

**REFUSING TO MAKE WAVES IS NOT AN INDICATOR OF A LIFE WELL LIVED.**

Their soul lacks backbone. For many, avoidance of life-affirming risk and terror of rejection makes them appear emotionally stilted and spiritually cold, even though, deep inside, they desperately want to know others and be known by them. Aleksandr Solzhenitsyn tapped into this hidden pain when he asked, "If one is forever cautious, can one remain a human being?"[1]

In the parable of the talents (Matthew 25), Jesus characterized fearful living as a kind of criminal behavior—as a crime against oneself, against one's neighbor, and against that person's ability to draw close to God. Wrote Henri Nouwen,

You need a lot of trust to give yourself fully to someone else. . . . Many people . . . simply don't want to make waves and instead go along with the trend. That is not obedience. That is adaptation.[2]

Refusing to make waves is not an indicator of a life well lived. Refusing to make waves is the state that precedes drowning.

# PASSING IT ON

The problem of timid living is perpetuated with the creation of timid children. Ominous research tells us that today's kids are more timid, risk-averse, and anxiety-ridden than past generations. Fear, my fellow parents, is our newest baby-sitter, our most prominent child-care consultant. The reasons are many, but one of the most misunderstood and underreported is our nation's most pervasive preoccupation: overprotective parenting.

We coaches call them "helicopter parents," because they constantly hover, and man, do they know how to attack. Most have no idea how their micromanaging hurts their kids behind the scenes, in the locker room, on the bench. By taking everything into their own hands and trying to make life smooth and painless, parents are preventing children from developing the abilities they need to actualize their potential. In the blunt words of Hara Estroff Marano:

> With few challenges all their own, kids are unable to forge their creative adaptations to the normal vicissitudes of life. That not only makes them risk-averse, it makes them psychologically fragile, riddled with anxiety. In the process they're robbed of identity, meaning and a sense of accomplishment, to say nothing of real happiness. Forget, too, about perseverance, not simply a moral virtue but a necessary life skill. These turn out to be the spreading psychic fault lines of the 21st-century youth. Whether we want to or not, we're on our way to creating a nation of wimps.[3]

Ten years ago or so, college counseling centers primarily helped students cope with roommate conflict and adjustment to college life. "No more," writes Marano.

The vast majority of the nation's college counseling centers report they are under siege, trying to meet the demands of unprecedented numbers of students with a range of serious psychological problems. From major and manic depression to eating disorders to self-harm to substance abuse, campus mental health centers are increasingly dealing with conditions that have life and death consequences.[4]

Jean Twenge, psychology professor at San Diego State University, says today's average child reports more anxiety than child psychiatric patients did fifty years ago.[5] "These are not the children of Beirut, or Israel's Haifa, or of Afghanistan," writes Patricia Pearson of USA Today. "These are American kids being terrified of math tests and bicycles."[6]

Today's children are taking longer to become adults—creating a new term for us to ponder, "adultescence." Some never do. In 1960, 77 percent, by age thirty, met the benchmarks for adulthood, such as living outside their parents' home, financial independence, and getting married. By 2000, the number had fallen to an alarming 46 percent.[7] Kids today are more psychologically troubled than kids have ever been.

Why are the world's most privileged kids running into unprecedented levels of mental illness and emotional distress? More than anything else, it's parental concern gone haywire. Explains psychologist Madeline Levine, author of *The Price of Privilege: How Parental Pressure and Material Advantage Are Creating a Generation of Disconnected and Unhappy Kids:*

Parents are genetically programmed to protect their children from threats. . . . Thankfully, the more recent historical threats to our children's well-being—malnutrition and devastating childhood illnesses—have been eradicated, or greatly reduced. Yet levels of parental anxiety remain extraordinarily high.[8]

Fearful parents are raising fear-filled children, which yields anxiety-saturated households and worry-worn relationships. Small wonder then that studies, like the one reported in *Time* on Father's Day 2006, show parents as less happy interacting with their own children than when "eating, exercising, shopping or watching television." Sadly, "the act of parenting makes most people about as happy as an act of housework."[9]

Consider the children of what we affectionately refer to as the Greatest Generation—my parents' generation. They lived through the Great Depression and fought in World War II. My father, who grew up in a poorer part of Dublin, remembers not having enough to eat. He remembers brushing his teeth with fine ash from the fireplace because they couldn't afford toothpaste. He took outdoor cold-water showers with a garden hose, in frigid winter. He brought his dead baby sister, wrapped in a white table-cloth, down to the cemetery because his own father was too distraught to manage the task. "I can still feel her cold body in my arms," he said, in a rare moment of emotional vulnerability.

My father possessed a level of serenity I wish I owned. I grew up on his stories, fed on them like baby crackers, and my children were changed by them as well. My oldest boy recently told me his grandfather's stories caused him to form a New Year's resolution: no longer to complain about petty things.

If only I were so mature. I'm ashamed at times of the issues I worry about in my life and in the lives of my three privileged children. Dad's generation exhibited very little fear of bodily injury or death in childhood, this when young death was more common, which he well knew. When surveyed in 1933, children did exhibit fear of "the supernatural and the dark."[10] These are normal childhood fears—contemporary kids have them as well. I'm sure you'll agree that if these were the only fears our children revealed to us at bedtime, we'd consider ourselves blessed indeed.

# THE "CHRISTIAN COMPONENT"

Here's a huge part of the problem: Christians are raising some of our culture's wimpiest kids. I don't say that they're becoming wimpy because we're teaching them to be humble and training them to embrace patience. They're going out into the world as wimps because we parents are ignoring the broader counsel of God, pushing away character traits that make us uncomfortable and pretending that being disengaged from the world is actually about holiness and purity, when more often it's about fear and a lack of love.

Many of us have been following a set of principles that's incomplete at best. This worldview, this outlook, is no one person's creation. It's no one denomination's fault. It's handed down from one seminary student to the next. It's what ministers are told is the central thrust of their faith, the main principles to emphasize on any given Sunday. It's what many of us have believed makes us believers. I call it The Official Script.

The Official Script likewise ignores God's broader council, lopping off entire facets of truth about how life is meant to be lived—about what our heart and mind are to become, and about the choices our will is to make. I can't overstress this: Usually our human intentions in all of this are for the absolute best. Nevertheless, by whatever name we call this way of life—Fortress Faith, Barricade Belief, Castle Christianity, Ivory-Tower Idealism—what we're actually doing is replacing love with fear, goodwill with criticism, joy with anxiety, hope with worry, and strength with silence.

We're often either marginalizing or largely eradicating such rugged virtues as shrewdness, boldness, and courage. These aspects of integrity require an active and assertive approach toward life—but many Christians think being assertive is wrong. As a result, we're bringing up our kids to be so sweet and compliant that I wouldn't be surprised if the federal government and armed forces commissioned studies to determine whether or not children who grew up in churches are capable of defending our country.

A football coach at a Christian high school told me it can take the better part of a season to convince his players that it's okay to try hard in competing against your opponent. "Many think it's wrong to," he says, rolling his eyes. "Some of these boys think it's wrong to tackle another person. Some of them I'll never convince otherwise."

Why would teenage males believe it's wrong for them to compete? Why would school kids believe it's wrong for them to set a boundary against an aggressive child or to be proactive and defend someone being bullied? One primary reason is that we're not showing them all of Jesus—in fact, sometimes we're showing them a false Jesus.

Read the Gospels, and you see that, yes, Jesus is the Lamb who was offered as a sacrifice for us. But read Revelation, too; do we know and remember that He's also the Lion, God's Ultimate Warrior? He is always and forever the same, yet on the day He returns, no one will be lulled to sleep with talk of "gentle Jesus, meek and mild."

Jesus *is* meek—He said so himself. Meekness *is* synonymous with yielding and being submissive. But do we ever pause to ask ourselves, *What is Jesus meek toward?* We cannot read the Gospels and conclude that He was submissive to the **MEEKNESS ISN'T FALSE HUMILITY, MEEKNESS ISN'T TIMIDITY, AND MEEKNESS ISN'T TERROR OF CONFLICT.** will of man, which is always tainted with self-interest and is sometimes wicked. *Jesus is submissive to His Father's will.* This is our calling, as well, and it's what we should be teaching our children.

Meekness isn't false humility, meekness isn't timidity, and meekness isn't terror of conflict. Meekness is knowing who we are, believing that what God says is true, and then submitting to Him in obedience because we love Him in response to His love for us.

Overall, that's not what our children are receiving from us. We're sending our children out onto life's daily battlefield in *fear*. How can we justify this? Most of us haven't been justifying it, at least not consciously; however, we're not thinking about what it will mean for them, for now and for the future. Often we haven't even yet realized what it means for *us*—that we're teaching our kids to be anxious and worried because *we* are.

Making matters worse is how one study shows that 85 percent of people who attend church possess what can be described as a passive personality. Such people are already too nice, yet they hear sermons that encourage them to be even nicer and more pleasant. For many, it's the wrong prescription, like giving birth control to a diabetic. Passive people already play life too safe, and they go to churches that tell them to play life even safer, producing children who are even more in love with safety than the risk that accompanies genuine faith and purposeful and intentional living.

When we're handcuffed, bound by shame or terror or condemnation or bitterness, lacking a true moral compass and a genuine strength, we naturally relate to our sons and daughters from that vantage point. We can learn to step forward and seek freedom and fullness, or we can stay self-absorbed and timid; either way, we're teaching them how to live. We can bless them with what they need to live abundantly, or we can rob them by withholding what they must have to grow up and live as the men and women the Lord made them to be.

# RAISING KIDS OF CHARACTER

This book shows parents how to raise assertive—not passive or aggressive—children who are able to live abundant lives and are better able to love God and others as they love themselves. It also shows parents who have already created dangerously submissive children what they can do to repair the damage.

For some, encouraging kids to be more ruggedly righteous and to embrace virtues like tough self-love and tough other-love is a frightening mandate that borders on (and even crosses over into) unchristian behavior. The opposite is true. Furthermore, I'm not advocating the development of children who are selfish and mean—again, just the opposite.

I want to offer thoughtful, practical advice on how to raise a new class of children who are well-schooled in assertive living and are more likely to become powerful and redemptive forces for good. Children who become adults better able to handle their own tears and to help dry the tears of this world. Children who throughout their lives can love their neighbor and "encourage the timid and help the weak" (1 Thessalonians 5:14) through sharing their strength and goodness.

I'll talk about what happens to kids when they're overprotected and underexposed. I'll give examples of adolescents who weren't allowed to develop or learn how to function in society. I'll examine the specter of bullying as it impacts and damages victims, bullies, parents, and the culture at large. I'll share my experiences of both bullying and being bullied, and how I've grown to overcome them in seeking to become a protector. And I'll demonstrate how our lack of courage and boldness is an ongoing travesty that we, together, can choose to turn into a triumph.

Also, I hope this book is powerful and helpful in exposing and combating the devastation caused by mistaking niceness for goodness. As I explained in both *No More Christian Nice Guy* and *Married . . . But Not Engaged,* what many of us consider to be manners or decorum, or being pleasant and considerate, is actually fear and passivity. This is vice disguised as virtue, and until we call it what it is and begin changing our belief and practice, we will carry this deception into our parenting, just as we carry it every-where else.

Many are entering the fray, picking up their swords and raising their voices against the tides of both culture and church that weaken rather than empower us and our children. George Barna, in his provocative work *Revolution,* calls such people "revolution-aries." A revolutionary might "feel like the odd person out" and be "embarrassed by language that promises Christian love and holiness but turns out to be all sizzle and no substance."[11]

I think Barna's right. I call these people "Second Circlers"— they're people of orthodox faith who live out that faith differently than the majority. And I think our numbers are growing. I am no longer able to warm myself by the fires burning in the center of our institutions of faith like I once did. I can no longer hold my tongue on what I've consistently experienced: earnest messages, delivered with charisma and zeal, whose content dissipates when taken out of the Petri dish of evangelical culture, dying quickly when exposed to the air of real life.

It doesn't matter how long information or exhortation has been around if it isn't true. Conventional thinking in itself isn't bad; we don't reject something for being conventional, but we must reject something that's both conventional and wrong. I have believed many well-meant pulpit falsehoods, and I've tried to live them out even when reality screamed another solution. I have suf-fered for lack of wisdom, and I don't want others, especially our children, to suffer the same results.

# ABOUT ME

I'm a card-carrying malcontent caught somewhere between the coldness of secular thinking and the wishful thinking of church culture. I have children's best interests in mind. I've been a father for fifteen years, and I've worked with children as a coach for more than ten. I love kids, and I want them to fare well in the real world. I want them to fulfill their dreams and potential. I want them to walk hand in hand with God, to understand that nothing can separate them from His love. I want them to experience the strength of heart and clearness of mind that come from genuine humility.

I want our daughters to know in the core of their soul that they are loved by God and valued by man. I want our sons to know in the core of their soul that they have what it takes to make it in life. I want our children to have the fortitude to persevere, the courage to create deep and abiding love, and the will to undergo the difficult work that dirties the hands of fighters for peace and justice.

I want our children to be remarkable and better than before. Not just better as in better manners, with more "pleases" and "thank-you's." Better as in defending the small classmate who's always getting his head smashed into lockers and ridiculed on MySpace. Better as in befriending the one who gets cliqued out or mocked because she wears last year's shoes or her hairstyle is six months behind the fashion curve. Better as in being less accepting of, and less silent about, what's really wrong and unacceptable in life. These children laugh more, play more, and weep more—they're emotionally attuned, spiritually vital, and pragmatically prepared to respond when virtue calls them to action.

One day a man, fishing by a river, sees small boys and girls caught in the current, struggling to keep their heads above the surface. He jumps in and does what he can to save them. He rescues some, he loses others . . . and they keep coming. Cold, exhausted, bewildered, and outraged, he charges upstream to find the source. A few miles up he sees a dump truck with the words "Good Intentions" on the side. It's chartered by parents releasing their children into adult life. They think they've given them the training necessary to swim well, and they're stunned by the catastrophe of the maiden voyage. There's weeping, dismay, and plenty of finger-pointing, mostly in the wrong direction. The laments at the beginning of the chapter remind us that such desperation is all around us; my desire, my heart, is to be one of those trying to stop all this.

The Bible says that the righteous are as bold as lions (Proverbs 28:1). However, what most kids learn in Sunday school is that the righteous are as sweet as pie. It's high time we side with God's Word instead—for our own good, for our children and grandchildren's good, and for the good of our nation.

# WHAT HAPPENED TO COURAGE AND INTEGRITY?

Marital disintegration often creates fragile, timid, and wary children. If they ever had it at all, the parental strength they once relied upon to help them face their inner insecurities and outerworld concerns becomes disrupted and usually dismantled. Sometimes their fragility is concealed behind a fake toughness; what's not hidden is a closed spirit that requires special healing to reopen.

Pop star Kelly Clarkson, who experienced this kind of homelife distress, wrote a dark and accusatory song that resonates in the hearts of many young adults who find themselves in a similar place. Her "Because of You" video shows a husband and wife at each other's throats while a little girl watches. After verbal brawls, depression, breakage, and tears, the father moves out.

Clarkson is that brokenhearted little girl. The song's poignant and painful chorus says that because of her parents' choices, she stays on the safe side of life, has a hard time trusting herself and others, and lives in constant fear. In an online interview she admitted it was hard for her family to watch the video, but she says "Because of You" is more than a protest. "The song is about breaking that cycle [of domestic violence and divorce] and not carrying it on to the next generation. Kids are like sponges, and they imitate what they see. And sometimes that's not fair because what we see is not good for us."[1]

It's a phenomenal tragedy that divorce rates in the church aren't markedly different from those in the general culture. At the same time, in recognizing the damaging effects of divorce and in seeking to stem its prevalence, the Christian community is among the few brave entities to confront the nefarious effects of divorce upon individuals and societies.

We need to learn how to start showing courage in other ways as well. Christian culture is prone toward "bubble living," isolating (or thinking we're isolating) ourselves from danger when sometimes what we're really doing is trying to immunize against living real life.

We're good at focusing on the negative: Jesus did say we're not to be of the world. Yet we somehow manage to forget the positive: we also are to be in it (see John 17). Failure to recognize and apply this—indeed, many Christians seek to live out the opposite—contributes to the crisis of fragile and ill-prepared children. If they're sealed in a biosphere for eighteen years, sure, they may stay "uninfected" . . . until they're let out. Then, far from being immunized or inoculated, they're prone to catch almost anything.

I'm still amazed by what I saw kids from Christian homes do when they got to college, away from their highly sheltered lives. They had professed to follow the Lord and receive His whole council, and they had lived such highly prescribed lives, but if their parents only knew half their exploits, they might, like Job, tear their clothing and sit in ashes. "Every fall," observes John Portmann, professor of religious studies at the University of Virginia, "parents drop off their well-groomed freshmen, and within two or three days many have consumed a dangerous amount of alcohol and placed themselves in harm's way. These kids have been controlled for so long, they just go crazy."[2]

It's not my intent to motivate change through scare tactics—that would be unfair, as well as ineffective. At the same time, one thing that should motivate us as parents is the vision of what our kids are becoming and will become if we continue in the same flawed direction instead of changing course. In many cases, parents are already so fearful and so controlling that kids and teens no longer share any of their real issues; they use chemicals, fantasy worlds, secret lives, and even self-mutilation in desperate attempts to cope with their unprecedented levels of psychological tension.

Most of them were taught at an early age that their interpretations of and feelings about the things around them were bad and wrong. They learned that certain emotions weren't allowed or acceptable; some were even punished for expressing certain thoughts and feelings. Their internal lives—that part of themselves that's supposed to help guide them into adulthood—has been hijacked by parents who have not allowed them to feel, think, process, and decide for themselves.

They tend to come from homes where distress and conflict are rarely, if ever, resolved well. From homes where too much of the usual messiness of family life was swept under the rug. Worst of all, some of this was done with spiritual pretense, or more accurately, spiritual excuse, to avoid the discomfort that comes from effective conflict resolution.

## MAJORING IN MINORS

By and large, we're not debilitating our kids on purpose. Over the years I've slogged through a ton of negativity, and I'm insistent that *guilt* is *not* an acceptable synonym for *parenthood*. Nonetheless, often with the best of intentions, Christian and non-Christian

NO MORE JELLYFISH, CHICKENS, OR WIMPS

parents alike are raising children who are passive, pleasant, and malleable rather than innovative, proactive, and bold. These "nice" children prevalently struggle with fear, anxiety, loneliness, and, later in life, relational instability and divorce. Our goal should be to create confident and truly virtuous kids who are capable of doing more than their part in obtaining an abundant life. These children become adults who lend their strength to others and help them obtain happiness as well.

**CHRISTIAN AND NON-CHRISTIAN PARENTS ALIKE ARE RAISING CHILDREN WHO ARE PASSIVE, PLEASANT, AND MALLEABLE RATHER THAN INNOVATIVE, PROACTIVE, AND BOLD.**

I have coached soccer for both genders, mostly boys, for more than a decade. Some are home-schooled, most go to public school, and some come from private schools. The kids from religious homes are mostly Christian, some Jewish, or a mixture of religious expressions and beliefs. Some don't go to a house of worship at all.

The only consistent difference I've noticed is that the kids who come from religious homes might swear less. *If my kid doesn't curse,* we say to ourselves, *I'm doing well.* In that one sense, this does make them different, but in the larger picture of life, it's a pathetic difference. Talk about straining at gnats and swallowing entire camels! (See Matthew 23:24.)

Jesus used this metaphor to describe errors the religious leaders of His day were perpetrating. They paid too much attention to minor matters and in the process ignored "weightier" matters like "justice, mercy, and good faith." I sometimes do the same thing as a parent, and I'm not proud of the reason: I strain at gnats because in myriad ways it's easier than teaching and living out for my kids a Christlike example of what matters most.

Swearing is the gnat some schools strain as well. My old high school, for example, held a summit among teachers and staff and decided that in the entire galaxy encapsulating tumultuous youth—which includes bullying so pervasive that an estimated 160,000 U.S. kids each day skip school—curtailing swearing was the most important crackdown they could undertake.

I'm not advocating swearing, especially taking the Lord's name in vain. But instead of a primary emphasis on rearing children known for not swearing as much as their peers, what about producing children known for their love of justice? Children who, with this love, are trained in the shrewd ways of creating righteousness and peace? What about rearing warriors of light, the kind of kids with fortitude and perseverance to withstand the wicked peer pressure that pounds them and others? Give kids *this* kind of upbringing, and issues like swearing may well just take care of themselves. After all, Jesus said it's what comes out of us that defines us and can defile us; a heart that produces blessedness and light cannot continue to produce profanity and darkness (Mark 7:14–23; Luke 6:44–46).

# GENTLE STRENGTH

Here's another difference I've seen as a coach, and it's heartbreaking. Religious kids are far more inhibited than their secular peers, and in the wrong way. They're less likely to put up a healthy boundary against another kid. They're also less likely to defend another person, and most of them have been drilled from toddlerhood that all conflict is wrong.

Conflict-avoidance disguised as "patience" or "gentleness" is a false front; the vice of cowardice is frequently disguised behind a "forbearing spirit" and a false understanding of gentleness. A gentle person uses the appropriate amount of force and power. When gentleness needs to take a stance, it does, and it does so with grace. But gentleness is always truthful, as well; niceness favors pleasantry and manners over truth. Niceness is the drowning of force (sometimes a good thing), but it can also be the refusal to honor what's right, the unwillingness to stand tall for any and all reasons.

The understanding that a gentle man still wields force is an eye-opening revelation to many men at my conferences, a revelation that often propels them into more godly living. Learning to use appropriate force in any given situation takes time and a cultivation of virtue. Trace the origin of the word *virtue* and you'll see that one of its meanings is "force": Virtue brings whatever energy and force is needful to a situation.

> **THE BELIEF THAT *NICE* EQUALS *GOOD* IS AMONG THE MOST AMAZING DECEPTIONS OF OUR TIME.**

The belief that *nice* equals *good* is among the most amazing deceptions of our time, and it's resulted in profound spiritual and relational degeneration as we've continued to atrophy behind the façade.

# COURAGE IS NONNEGOTIABLE

What has happened to make parents discount the more muscular virtues, such as courage and integrity? These are obtained, sculpted, and bolstered by far more than requiring our children to say "Yes ma'am" and "Thank you" when receiving a cookie at Aunt Thelma's. And so much more than memorizing verses or reciting prayers.

We think that children of integrity, first and foremost, do not lie; this focuses on the negative. The larger trait of integrity, *posi-*

*tively,* requires them to tell the whole truth. The difference in character is enormous (more on this in chapter 11).

As Christians, we've been told and taught that we build integrity and character by avoiding sin. Part of that answer (the negative) is right, but in overlooking the other half (the positive), we sell our kids down Good Intentions River, which runs through each state and county in the nation. Jesus warned that the abundant life He offers is hard to find (Mark 10:24–25); we unintentionally make it harder to find, distancing our children from it by training them to focus on avoiding mistakes instead of living boldly and righteously. Possessing integrity and character is far more than checking off lists of do's and don'ts.

Courage, also known as fortitude, is the ability to confront fear, pain, danger, uncertainty, or intimidation, whether for ourselves or for others. Courage, one of the four "cardinal virtues" (along with wisdom, temperance, and justice) is pivotal, because in order to possess *any* virtue, truly, a person must be able to sustain it in the face of difficulty. This is why Winston Churchill called courage the "first of human qualities . . . because it guarantees all the others."

Courage is the foundational virtue upon which others rest. Or don't.

I believe we have avoided and minimized this dimension of character, in part, to settle our internal rumblings about our lack of virtue. Senator John McCain, former prisoner of war and author of *Why Courage Matters: The Way to a Braver Life,* implies that we set the bar for "courage" almost on the ground, just so we can think and say that we have it: "We say it takes courage to be different from the mainstream in our preferences in fashion, music, the length and color of our hair."[3]

And, he says, we are not teaching our children what this foundational virtue really is.

If children are taught that simply being honest or doing

the best they can or appreciating what they have without complaint is considered by their society to be an act of courage, will they be more or less motivated to summon the real thing in a crucible?[4]

We know the answer to McCain's rhetorical question even if we don't want to admit it. His guidance for parents is even more pointed:

> Parents who want their children to have courage usually think of it in its physical expression first, and they try to impart it to them by experience and encouragement. When they fall from the horse we've set them upon, we'll encourage them to get back in the saddle. Don't be afraid of the ball, we tell them, trust your reflexes and your glove. Don't give up, keep trying, you'll get better. These are, of course, sensible encouragements to a child. They need to be so encouraged. But we're not exactly teaching them courage. We're teaching them physical skills. We're teaching them to be strong. We're helping them acquire fortitude. We're building their confidence and giving them hope. These are elements of courage in most instances, but not the whole virtue. Their effect alone might only be to give them daring, nerve. They might grow up and climb mountains or become risk-taking entrepreneurs. Not necessarily bad things. But is that all we think courage is? Is that what we're trying to teach them? Without other instruction, they could turn out to be Enron executives. They had daring, to be sure. But they lacked ethics. They lacked a sense of honor, and they lacked courage.[5]

Here's another way of thinking about this issue: How often do we diagnose a behavior as cowardice? For instance, what do you say after your son tells you about a bullying he witnessed and didn't intervene, just stood there with the group? Have you helped him figure out that the sludge-like feeling gumming up his soul is a result of cowardice? Do you explain that cowardice is a normal but insufficient response to seeing someone unjustly treated or cruelly humiliated? Do you teach him that being wise and acting thoughtfully does *not* mean he is also to remain frozen, inert, and innocuous?

For some, the shame of cowardice upon their soul, mind, and heart lasts forever. Writes street evangelist Truxton Meadows:

> I'm forty years old. And I've lived a lot of life and made many mistakes. I have regrets but have reconciled them in my life. The only nagging regrets I still have that I can't reconcile are the times that I could have stood up for a kid that was getting bullied and I didn't. I was small and got picked on myself so I didn't want to draw the bully's attention and sometimes joined in to fit in. I regret that I never stood up for myself and others. [e-mail to author]

Many parents have never even had a conversation with their children about cowardice. Warning against its corrosive nature isn't even usually on our parental radar, or included in many sermons. Instead, most of us are quick to warn our kids to avoid getting too involved (or involved at all) when someone is mistreated because of the collateral damage it may do to them. *This is in direct defiance to how Jesus told us to live* (see the parable of the good Samaritan in Luke 10). And we're overlooking the far-reaching damage of cowardice itself: Ultimately, cowardice can be as destructive as drug addiction.

We don't discuss how cowardice undermines our integrity and character, much less what God says about it. There are approximately thirty biblical examples of cowardice, and every one is a cautionary tale.

**MANY PARENTS HAVE NEVER EVEN HAD A CONVERSATION WITH THEIR CHILDREN ABOUT COWARDICE.**

Are you aware that even in many countries (such as France and Germany), civil courage is enforced by law? That if citizens witness a public crime they are obliged to act, either by alerting the authorities or by intervening? Or if the crime is committed in a private environment, witnesses are either to report it or try to stop it?

*We don't talk about cowardice with our children because we don't really think courage is all that necessary in the first place.* We also can't bear the thought that our kids might exhibit cowardice. In fact, in this area, we'd rather be ignorant or uninvolved than engage the matter and help our sons and daughters go to work on it. We're more worried about hurting our children's feelings than we are concerned about cultivating hearts that don't listen to fear when making decisions. (We'll later explore this pivotal issue in greater depth.)

# WE'RE *ALL* IN THIS

Just to be clear, there are no stones in my hand. I've either committed all the parental sins I'll address or I've thought about committing them. This book isn't about blame. It's about reform and turning away from beliefs, practices, and trends that hurt our kids and our culture.

We all make mistakes, partly because going into parenting at first means going in somewhat blind. Most of us get (or at least feel) sucker-punched now and again. Even the experts, like Sally Shaywitz, MD, neuroscientist and author:

> When my children were growing up, I was a very young and inexperienced mother. I believed everything had to be perfect. It seemed to matter so much that they were each in the right classes, did well in school, participated in sports activities, and took music lessons. Today, with the advantage of hindsight, I would be so much more laid-back and relaxed. I certainly would have more faith in my children's innate strengths.[6]

Like Mary Pipher, PhD, psychologist and author:

I erred in the direction of trying a little too hard to make sure that they didn't suffer. If they were irresponsible and left something out in the rain, I was more than happy to help them replace it. I made sure that whatever mistakes they made didn't cost them too dearly. . . . So I'd cushion less and let them feel the full weight of their consequences more.[7]

Like William Damon, PhD, professor of education and author:

Rather than talk about our worries in front of the kids, we'd shelter them. So all they saw was the anxiety. Kids are smart, and ours knew their parents were worried. . . . There are some conflicts—such as marital—that you don't bring the kids into, but there's no need to completely shield them from everything. It strengthens kids to confront real life, especially if they confront it with your guidance.[8]

Or like Harold Koplewicz, MD, child and adolescent psychiatrist. He and his wife created

[a] hothouse orchid. Joshua is very sensitive to everything in a good and bad way. As a child, he felt every slight, separation, and bump in the road. Whenever something negative happened, we listened, empathized, and understood. However, we should also have helped him put things into perspective. This would have helped "toughen" him up and made it easier for him to adjust to experiences that won't go his way later in life.[9]

Without wishing ill on anyone, isn't it at least reassuring to know that the experts can also get it wrong? If you're like me, prone to self-flagellation or condemnation, I want to encourage you, instead, to begin using that energy toward charting a better course. When we're all racing in place on the same Tour de Fear hamster wheel, everybody loses—children *and* parents.

We're afraid of falling behind. We're worried our kids might not do as well as other kids. We're terrified that we'll fail, and that our children will grow up to be the everlasting proof of our inadequacy. Letting them learn and decide to make choices and take calculated risks *feels* wrong, broken somehow.

By living out of our fears, we've made parental panic culturally acceptable. But the apostle John, in proclaiming the truth of Jesus, makes clear that where love reigns, fear is clipped (see 1 John 4). Instead of building entire lives and families on a foundation of fear and frenzy, we can choose to equip and empower our sons and daughters for a future of fullness.

An anxious approach to life leads to an anxious life, a life prone to depression, instability, abuse, atrophy, and addiction. We need to look at the source of our parental anxiety, asking ourselves, which came first: deep-seated anxiety in kids, or overarching anxiety in parents? We also need to consider how our children can possibly fare well in life on their own if we persist in our unceasing advice, micro-structured decisions, and every-second protection.

Ultimately, kids need to learn how to fly, and we must ask: Just how strong can their wings get when they're never allowed to use them?

CHAPTER

3

# OVERPROTECTIVE PARENTS, UNDERDEVELOPED KIDS

*Steve wasn't prepared for adult life. This fact has been driven into him in part through his own troubled conscience; it's been driven in even more by his wife of eighteen years, fed up with being the only proactive adult in the home.*

*"She screams at me— 'Stephen, you're such an idiot, you don't know how to be a man!' " he told me.*

*"That must be hard to hear," I offered.*

*"It is, but it's true," he said.*

Steve got the double whammy, the full nice-guy childhood.[1] First, he lived a highly scripted life; his parents had micromanaged his childhood, too often overriding his will and fighting too many of his battles. Second, he got an angry God thrown at him—a God out to get him and ready to crush him at any moment if he messed up.

God was an angry taskmaster, who must always be appeased with good behavior, a sort of behavioral sacrifice. "God was constantly watching me and my siblings," Steve recalls. "He was always looking for us to screw up so he could punish us.

"You wouldn't dare think of eating without thanking God for your food, even during the times when I wasn't thankful. I had to pretend a lot in my prayers."

Steve says his home created solemn people who worried they were not in the "palm of God's will." He laments, "I just never felt comfortable with God or with myself. Or at school. I was constantly second-guessing myself, the way my parents did. Their prayers were often one big worry session."

Steve wasn't allowed to select his own clothing or choose the color of his own room. His friends were handpicked by his parents. His mom determined his hairstyle even into high school.

None of this paved any paths for him to make friends or get along with others. He says now, "I was a snot. I put a lot of rules on games back then, so I can see why kids didn't want to play with me. Playing with me wasn't play. It was work. Kids needed a manual in order to play with me."

**STEVE'S MOM THOUGHT SHE WAS BEING A GOOD MOTHER, BUT HER INTERVENTION MADE MATTERS WORSE.**

Once in elementary school he was painfully reminded of this when the other kids excluded him from dodge ball, gobbling up all the balls in the playground's equipment shed. Then he wanted his own ball to bounce around, and his overprotective mom sprung into action. "Soon I was given a brand-new rubber ball with large initials written on it in black permanent ink." But in the world of children, she may as well have written "LOSER" instead of Steve's initials. Steve's mom thought she was being a good mother, but her intervention made matters worse. "Kids ridiculed me even more. I didn't want the

ball. I kicked it into a neighbor's backyard when no one was looking."

As an adult, Steve looks to his wife to make the decisions in
their marriage.[2] She's the driving force, and her drive is weakening. She's tired from having to do almost all the daily lifting. Steve
was conditioned to wait on others to make decisions for him; he's
passive, and he's never developed the ability to make choices.
Steve has *learned* how to be helpless and reactionary due to overprotection. Growing up, he wasn't allowed even limited dominion
over expression of who he was. Small decisions, such as what kind
of books he could read, or what he wanted to do on a Saturday
afternoon, were made for him. Or more accurately, against him.
His will was hijacked by his parents and by what he was told God
wanted him to do.

And there's Max. Max's mom had a difficult upbringing that
included physical and emotional abuse. She vowed that when she
became a mother she would not perpetuate the same mistakes—
she wanted her son to experience none of the pain she'd endured.
Unfortunately, she failed to see the difference between debilitating suffering and the kind of day-to-day distress that gradually
teaches children how to thrive in the real rough-and-tumble
world.

They lived in relative ease and privilege, but Max's mom lived
as though every object and idea in existence could (and would)
harm him. Her campaign to scrub his world of discomfort began
when he was a newborn. She would search the inside of his sleep-
ers for an imperfect seam. Anything with the hint of a rough spot
was rejected and thrown away.

She verbally horsewhipped neighborhood kids if they hurt his
feelings. She soon became known as the "crazy lady" up the
street. If he had a complaint about a class, she was there in a

moment, telling the teacher how bad she was at her job. She was the kind of mom educators love to see leave their school, the kind that makes good teachers leave the profession.

She had in her mind an immature mantra: Protect my son at all costs. And sadly, at least for a while, she succeeded—she smothered him. Her overprotective approach toward motherhood is reminiscent of Truman Capote's epigraph in his last, unfinished work: "More tears are shed over answered prayers than unanswered ones."

Her protection further isolated Max from the world of boys and men, who found him odd and his company distasteful. He didn't act like a man in the making. Nor did he show much interest. He hung out on the sidelines of life, rarely saying or doing anything of substance. He dropped out of high school and sold drugs.

Max doesn't remember being disciplined, and so he never acquired self-discipline. He also didn't receive any parental consequences for his increasing criminal behavior. Neighbors complained, "Has anyone ever told him the word *no*?" Max was a product of his age, of good-intentioned parenting that followed this contemporary belief: Good self-esteem comes from always feeling good about yourself, from never feeling pain or discomfort, from having every potential risk screened and eliminated before it reaches you.

Obsessive hyper-management was like a moniker on a sweater: Good Mother. You could see it in her eyes and in her stride when she swooped into action on behalf of her son, the project into which she funneled her fears. She believed that the wake forming behind her—roiling with belligerence and insults upon those misfortunate enough to receive her abuse—was clearing the way to a brighter future for her only child.

Hers weren't just everyday run-of-the-mill battles, the kind that make up the usual grind of life. From the tone in her voice, the resolve in her eyes, and purposeful heaviness in her stride, she seemed to see herself as a present-day Joan of Arc. Hers was a crusade: Good Versus Evil. How could anyone reproach such earnestness, such fervor, such seeming nobility?

But there was another reason she behaved this way. She needed her boy to fill a void in her. She was lonely. Because she ate through the goodwill of others, she burned through friends; however, Max wasn't a flight risk. His dependency upon her made him a willing captive, a slave to her unmet desires, a needed companion to stave off the hell of isolation through the sin of emotional incest.

The current result of her hovering and bullying parental philosophy? Max is addicted to heroin, is in and out of prison, and sleeps in his car. He, like her, is fragile, broken, and depleted. He was overprotected, and now he is undernourished and underdeveloped. His scars, as with all emotional and spiritual scars, still contain wisdom and hard-to-decipher signposts pointing the way back to wholeness. Yet he doesn't have the skills, perseverance, or courage to unearth them, study them, learn from them, and repent—he has no idea how to proactively turn away from lies and toward truth. He needs a soul transplant.

# A MOST WELL-INTENTIONED DISASTER

Countless other men and women have grown up under overprotection, the new societal mandate for stressed-out and nervous parents. It's a culture full of round-the-clock worrying, consistent second-guessing, nocturnal teeth grinding, and coffee-drenched mornings. It's where we run to find quick answers and complete solutions to any little problem our children face; we do this whenever we have little or no faith that the issue could be worked out over time and doesn't need our constant attention and intervention. Where we speed down to our child's school and bring them their homework assignments and books because they accidentally left them at home, instead of letting reality sink in, teach, and minister. Where parents pay their children money every time they win a game. Where parents call coaches and chew them out because their child didn't make the team. Where kids aren't allowed to play on safe streets because parents are freaked out about kidnapping. This fiasco can be at its worst in the churches where parents receive high praise for sequestering their children from the world.

Many men, like me, struggle with parenting that smothers, though women are front-lining the charge in this obsession with riding roughshod over children. Says Hara Estroff Marano,

> Women are leading the way, teaching men how to over-parent. Men, however, have their own reasons. They grew up realizing that they scarcely knew their fathers and are trying to overcompensate with their own children for what their fathers never were with them—involved.[3]

One reason women are in charge of this unfortunate conquest is found in Max's life. His mother had unfulfilled and frustrated romantic yearnings, energy from which is often channeled into hyper-parental vigilance, leading to highly enmeshed mother/son relationships that emasculate young men. Specifically, maternal overprotection leads to victimization: It is one of the most powerful predictors that the son will be picked on in school and that he will not offer resistance. When a boy's mother drastically eliminates his exploration of the world and vicariously fights his battles, he will be perceived as a victim—in particular, a passive victim.

Writes Dr. Debra Peplar, professor of psychology at York University:

> Maternal overprotection predicts victimization if during conflict children feel compelled to submit—and are also

afraid. If boys internalize the negative messages about themselves that are implied in the inept parenting of over-protection, and come to feel that Mother's wish is their command, then the boundaries with their mother are blurred.[4]

These parents:

▶ Interrupt their child often.

▶ Tell their child what to think and feel, even telling them that what they are currently thinking or feeling is wrong. (In Christian circles, they might be told, for example, that feeling anger is sinful.)

▶ Override their child's initiative.

▶ Abruptly change topics of conversation.

▶ Tell their child to change his/her facial expression.

▶ Are only willing to discuss certain issues.

Today's prevailing Christian worldview largely demands that a mother overprotect her sons, and she's often regarded as negligent if she doesn't. For a woman to raise a courageous child who has Christlike characteristics in his life, she must swim against the pre-dominant subcultural mainstream and allow him to take meaning-ful risks through which to grow and mature.

As we saw with Max's mom, loneliness is another common source for overprotection that carries with it the potential for overarching fear and degrees of paranoia. What's so slippery about such behavior? *It appears so sacrificial.* It's selfishness disguised as thoughtfulness.

Furthermore, a good desire to nurture, taken too far, can be far too much of a good thing. Here's Dr. James Dobson's gentle explanation:

From about three years of age, your little pride and joy begins making his way into the world of other people. . . . This initial "turning loose" period is often extremely threatening to the compulsive [often an overprotective] mother. Her natural reaction is to hold her baby close to her breast, smothering him in "protection." By watching, guarding, defending, and shielding night and day, perhaps she can spare her child some of the pain she herself experienced growing up. However, her intense desire to help may actually interfere with growth and development. Certain risks must be tolerated if a child is to learn and progress.[5]

Contrary to our assumptions, kids who receive constant parental protection don't do better in life. When they're too often harbored from inevitable hardships and challenges, they do not develop a keen understanding of their own abilities and weaknesses. Sometimes they become overconfident, possessing a distorted sense of themselves; most of the time they lack confidence, some to the brink of social anxiety and clinical depression, prime targets for childhood bullying that can persist into adulthood.

**CONTRARY TO OUR ASSUMPTIONS, KIDS WHO RECEIVE CONSTANT PARENTAL PROTECTION DON'T DO BETTER IN LIFE.**

These latter kids, over months and years of not being able to grow, have a vital life power gradually drained from them, making them unable to donate power to others and to live intentionally, redemptively. Some never fully recover. Others spend part or most of their adulthood "getting their life back," or rather, becoming themselves for the first time; many of these do so only after devastating blows like divorce, career chaos, or bankruptcy.

Whether overprotected children become arrogant (overconfident) or self-diminishing (under-confident), they share the same malady: they focus too much on themselves, and not enough on others. This is a basic component of narcissism; narcissists of all kinds are socially inept, repeatedly displaying behavior that breaks relational ties with others, pushing them further into the pit of isolation.

# KIDS NEED TO FEEL BAD SOMETIMES

If you want to shock contemporary sensibilities, tell today's parents that their little ones need to feel life's inevitable stings from time to time. Not the kind that crushes their spirit, but the kind that awakens their discernment, increases their understanding, and gives them wisdom about the realities of life. Explains child psychologist David Elkind, professor at Tufts University: "We learn through experience, and we learn through bad experiences. Through failure we learn how to cope."[6]

While speaking to parents about raising kids with successful character, Dr. Henry Cloud was asked: "If there's one thing that's most important to teach children about success, what would it be?"

"I would teach them how to lose," he said.

A woman tilted her head, looked at him strangely, and asked, "Why in the world would you want to teach them how to lose?"

"*Because they will,*" Cloud said emphatically.[7]

The most important lesson children gain from losing is that *the difference between winners and losers is not that winners never lose.*

The difference is that winners lose well, and losers lose poorly. As a result, winners lose less in the future and do not lose the same way that they lost last time, because they have learned from the loss and do not repeat the pattern.

But losers do not learn from what they did and *tend to carry that loss or pattern forward into the next venture, or relationship, and repeat the same way of losing.*[8]

This fundamental building block of successful living is being denied a growing number of children. In various ways, their parents are not allowing them to fail in a meaningful way. Not surprisingly, though, another dramatic venue for this burgeoning problem is schools. "Parents and schools are no longer geared toward child development, they're geared to academic achievement," says Elkind.[9] Some kids are "achieving" it over their teacher's warm resignation letter; parents are exhausting educators by "protecting" their children, and schools are furthering it by emphasizing test-score results over well-rounded students.

A study from Sydney, Australia, shows that principals as well as teachers are having difficulty handling a growing number of parents who are "aggressive, pestering, vexatious and unreasonable . . . who are hell-bent on getting their kids an educational edge and convinced beyond reason that their children are supremely gifted and talented. . . . The burnout rate for teachers in their first three to five years is as high as 30 percent, research shows."[10] The article says that one out-of-control mother, who refused to acknowledge that her child was a troublemaker, suggested that the school punish the student next to him, "because that would be enough to shock him into behaving." A University of Sydney study shows teachers leaving the profession in droves at about twenty-nine, only a few years out of college.

Some schools are accommodating our culture's belief that life's bumps and bruises should be eradicated from the lives of our children. An elementary school in Santa Monica, California, expresses a negative opinion of a game that it considers both physically dangerous and potentially harmful to a child's developing psyche. That game is tag.

"The running part of this activity is healthy and encouraged;

however, in this game, there is a 'victim' or 'it,' which creates a self-esteem issue."[11] Should we replace hide-and-seek with don't-find-me-too-quickly-or-I-might-feel-bad?

Nations far and wide are losing their nerve to truly help children succeed. Rod Morgan, a former professor of criminology and now chairman of the Youth Justice Board in England, says thousands of children are ending up in court because teachers are afraid to discipline students for bad behavior out of fear that *they* will be brought into court. Morgan is urging his country to rally around teachers who struggle to contain bad-behavior children—especially single-parent children.

> We know that the proportion of families where young parents—often mothers bringing up a child alone without the presence of a male role model and a father present on the scene, and without the support of an extended family—are having to cope with more and more challenging child behaviour in fairly deprived areas. This has to be confronted. Teachers have to be supported to explain the need for boundaries, to enforce boundaries, but to do it in a manner which remains inclusive and to do it in a more assertive manner for those parents who may collude with their own children's bad behaviour.[12]

It is a common mistake to hold on to the things we love too tightly. As with Max's mom, it can feel so noble and so right. But good intentions aside, the consequences of wrongly raising our kids can be deadly. It's not so much that we need to do more. It's that what we're doing needs to be different. We need to change course.

CHAPTER
4

# LINKS BETWEEN OVER-PARENTING AND SOCIAL DISASTER

The ability to plan resides in the prefrontal cortex, called the brain's executive branch. It is highly suspected that when this part of the brain is unable to regulate our usual thought patterns, depression kicks in. Intellectual rigor, which can be as complex as composing a symphony or as simple as writing down an accurate to-do list, helps form this portion of our brain. "It's in the setting of goals and progress in working toward them, however mundane they are, that positive feelings are generated. From such everyday activity, resistance to depression is born."[1]

The lonely and depressed adult sees success as something outside her control. She does not see herself as an active agent in the quality of her life. This is the thinking of learned helplessness, an unintended but tragic consequence endured by the person who had her life lived for her during her early years. When she's later released into what's supposed to be adulthood, she is vastly and painfully unprepared to take charge.

Remember what Henry Cloud said about allowing children to experience failure? Overprotected kids have their losses handled for them; later, when they face defeat and have no parental buffer, they attribute it to qualities within them that they perceive to be set in stone. They don't believe they can change—they assume they're inadequate, insufficient, not up to snuff . . . that they simply don't have what it takes, and that's that. They constantly internalize criticism from others and bury themselves under their own self-condemnation. They disregard external factors and turn inward, choosing "passive" over "proactive" and stunting their already profoundly stunted development. Because they're convinced they'll never measure up, never move forward, and never have a reason to hope for more, they don't acquire new skills, they don't change bad habits, and they don't learn to succeed. Because they're determined to live small, to avoid risk, and to focus on themselves, such people make inefficient employees and needy spouses.

Once upon a time, the group seeing the largest increase in depression was adults over forty. Depression is now rising among children, and it's striking them at younger and younger ages. Instead of progressively learning how to live fully and meaningfully, kids are becoming more worried and tentative and less able to grow through facing normal issues and conquering their challenges.

An anxious and fearful mindset is heavily linked to depression. Some kids, around 20 percent, *are* born with a more fearful predisposition than others. "They can be spotted in the womb; they have fast heartbeats. Their nervous systems are innately programmed to be over-excitable in response to stimulation, constantly sending out false alarms about what is dangerous."[2]

Already, as infants and children, these kids see threats where others don't. They tend to be shy, withdrawn, and lacking in social confidence; other kids see their vulnerability and often target them for bullying.

If this were the only information we had about such children, we might conclude that their lot in life was held in the cold hands of destiny and DNA. However, research shows that genetic programming *isn't* inevitable:

> At age two, none of the over-excitable infants wound up fearful if their parents backed off from hovering and allowed the children to find some comfortable level of accommodation to the world on their own. *Those parents who overprotected their children—directly observed by conducting interviews in the home—brought out the worst in them.*[3]

Says Michael Liebowitz, clinical professor and head of the Anxiety Disorders Clinic at New York State Psychiatric Institute:

> [Children] need to be gently encouraged to take risks and learn that nothing terrible happens. They need gradual exposure to find that the world is not dangerous. Having overprotective parents is a risk factor for anxiety disorders because children do not have opportunities to master their innate shyness and become more comfortable in the world.[4]
>
> This cuts down two false parental assumptions. The truth is, constant scrutiny leads anywhere but toward innate confidence or inner strength. It makes kids self-conscious and even self-obsessed. It teaches them to bury their feelings and to lie about the emotions they do experience. They come to feel they have no real choice in the matter: The message sent by constant scrutiny is that the "right" emotions are the ones their parents want them to express. This gradually paralyzes the growth of any child, and it can do untold damage to boys, who lag behind girls in emotional intelligence. Broad denial of emotions is one

reason today's teenagers can seem so absurd. Even though what they're hiding is in plain view, they feel they're better off pretending it isn't there—they're desperately trying to get out from under the magnifying glass.[5]

This treatment of children is usually well-meant but usually disastrous. It makes kids prone to some of the worst mental illnesses, and it weakens our social fabric by weakening young people to the point of cowardice. These children are more prone to follow destructive peer pressure, more susceptible to herd mentality, more passive against bullying and abuse, far less likely to defend another person, and unwilling to assert their will in questioning corrupt authority.

This last observation, an inability to recognize and differentiate between healthy and unhealthy authority, is particularly important to the work I do with passive men, whom I call Nice Guys. It can take them years to confront clear examples of workplace bullying or social abuse—some of which would likely be deemed illegal. When some never do confront it, they're filled with shame and self-reproach, but they've been trained (often through an overprotected childhood) to rationalize away their emotions and to simply accept abusive treatment. Their will, their conscience, their dreams and desires—their *being*—was so overridden for so long by hovering parents that they became programmed to accept anything and everything that comes their way.

## SOCIAL UN-TIES

Another pitfall of overprotection is a heartbreaking irony: Because over-parented children are taught to obsess over themselves, they don't learn how to connect with others. *Helicopter parents, who think they are drenching their children with love, are raising lonely sons and daughters.* The kids' constant self-focus, developed under the tonnage of unending parental intervention, handicaps them in every social setting.

Self-focused kids—whether they're shy and withdrawn or brash and mouthy—do not reach out to other people. They're not friendly, so they don't make friends well. Their near total self-consciousness appears to others as self-absorption. What they need is wise guidance and encouraging nudges. Problem is, that's exactly what many overprotective parents find distasteful and don't want—nudging their kids outward, even little by little, would negate their constant presence and persistent meddling.

And when they do allow their children to enter "the realm of others," by demanding special consideration, they expect others to coddle their child. They tend to unleash harsh words and passive-aggression on those who don't, whether grown-ups or youngsters. Such parents, mostly mothers, stack the deck against their own best interests as they contaminate play and turn their children into the pariahs of the kid world.

These lonely children tend strongly toward depression—again, they don't learn how to think and choose for themselves, and their brain gradually becomes more and more unable to manage their situations. Furthermore, though, because their parents' words

**KIDS WHO INTEGRATE WELL AND UNDERSTAND THE NUANCED WORLD OF PLAY GET INVITED TO PLAY WITH OTHER KIDS.**

and actions teach them that virtually everyone else is an enemy or an antagonist, they can also become unreasonably suspicious, or in a word, paranoid.

Timid, isolated kids see offense where no offense is given. For instance, an unintentional elbow in the back during recess is considered a calculated attack; the child who sees it that way is touchy, uppity . . . a potential wimp and a target for bullies. Kids who integrate well and understand the nuanced world of play get invited to play with other kids. Those who don't are excluded, overtly or covertly, and that dangerous cycle can form very early—experts say sometimes as early as three years of age.

Social ties not only keep us at healthy distances from the cliffs of depression and anxiety, they also keep us tethered to the real world, grounded in the sometimes-hard-to-ascertain state of reality, especially when we're under intense or prolonged stress. A good friend or network of friends can help keep us from sinking in many of life's deep ends.

In the long run, the ability to maintain social ties is probably the best kind of life and health insurance. "This has already become part of the wisdom of the culture. Medical studies tell us that having friends, even animal ones, improves physical health among [for example] the sick, the disabled, and the elderly."[6]


One aspect of our immune system is particularly relevant to the shy child. He or she seems, broadly, more attuned to picking up negative signals than positive ones. A mildly negative event, like a look of disapproval from a friend, registers far more strongly than moderately positive events, or even strongly positive ones.

Dr. John Gottman, of the Gottman Institute, has found that a single look of contempt can outweigh five good acts.[7] If this predisposition to taking predominantly negative feelings to heart is common in people generally, it's that much more so in the hypersensitive child, one who lives in a world filled with various degrees of fear. This not only puts her even further behind in life, it also places her squarely in the path of another devastating force for overprotected children: Their timid, helpless disposition and countenance throughout the school day means they're the kind of kids that attract bullies.

# BULLIED VICTIMS AND OVERPROTECTION

Child psychologist David Schwartz conducted a novel and amazing study of children drawn from eleven different schools, none of whom knew each other at the outset. He sorted them into thirty playgroups, each consisting of one popular, one neglected, two average, and two socially rejected boys. Then he silently monitored and with the use of hidden cameras videotaped them in a series of play sessions held on five consecutive days. Even in the first two sessions, before bully/victim situations developed, the children who showed themselves to be "victim kids" behaved submissively.

Victims were dangerously nonassertive before any confrontations began. And they didn't initiate conversation. "They made no attempts to influence or persuade (or dissuade!) their peers— no demands, requests, or even suggestions about how or what they should all play."[8] In common language, they let their peers walk all over them.

> [Victims] didn't ever take a leadership role with their peers, so their playmates rated them low on leadership. They were thoroughly socially incompetent and spent their time in passive play, playing parallel to and apart from their peers rather than with them.
>
> Even when in the first two sessions their peers approached them to engage in rough-and tumble play or to interest them in doing something, children who became victims responded wildly inappropriately. They shrank from the bid with submission, a show of pain, asking peers to stop, or simply yielding their position. Their play style wasn't just passive, it was inflexibly so; no matter how they were approached, they capitulated. Rough-and-tumble play, while it mimics aggressive action, is usually pro-social in nature. It is a good indicator of social competence

because it requires such complex skills as emotion regulation. Absent that, and the play can quickly turn into a battle—a smile becomes a snarl, a foot lands too hard, or someone misreads into the horsing-around a real intent to harm.[9]

Regarding bully-victim relationships on the whole, it's shocking that when they're asked, bullies express more contempt and disdain for their victims than victims do their bullies! Some victims can't even muster the outrage necessary to condemn the behavior. Why? You guessed it: Often their parents have commandeered their lives for so long that it doesn't feel normal to raise appropriate boundaries with others. Children who possess healthy self-regard (thinking neither too little nor too much about themselves) do not suffer from this problem. Most do not become victims.

We'll later explore more about the misunderstood world of victims and bullies, including other reasons kids become victims that aren't related to the theme of this chapter. For now, it's important we realize how overprotective parenting creates a destructive downward spiral of events.

## SUGGESTIONS FOR SHYNESS

Some shyness is good, for a kid and for an adult. Shyness can keep us from making fools of ourselves, and it can also stop us from hurting others. Without some level of social inhibition, we will tend to come across as overbearing. Shyness helps us formulate what we'll say and do beforehand, helping us to make wiser choices.

The downside, of course, is that too much shyness is excessive self-consciousness. The overly shy fall inward and cocoon themselves from the outside world, which struggles to understand them and connect with them. They can be lightning-quick to feel rejection, shame, and ridicule.

As a coach, I can tell you that shy kids demand more time, and often not in a good way. If a kid needs help because he's struggling with a concept, I'm glad to assist. But shy kids frequently aren't very teachable. Many rebuff attempts to learn something new because new concepts require risk in their execution. A coach (or a teacher) can end up repeatedly going over the same issue with limited results, occasionally spanning months or even years with no real improvement.

This tends to put them in a place of ill-standing with their peers. Their teammates or classmates, if healthy, won't resent them if they're genuinely seeking to learn, but if they're just flat-out needy or clingy, they set themselves apart from the other kids, who then get less instruction and attention. When it comes to growth and development, outside of specialized environments designed for children with particular needs, there comes a point where kids are expected to improve or be gradually and increasingly left behind.

Every leader—whether a pastor, teacher, administrator, or coach—needs parents alongside the kids in his charge. A coach can show a boy how to score the goal; Dad and Mom need to log the

**A COACH CAN SHOW A BOY HOW TO SCORE THE GOAL; DAD AND MOM NEED TO LOG THE ASSISTS.**

assists. A leader is allotted a certain amount of time and a certain number of resources to share with the kids he's leading; getting no help from a given home is likely to result in that kid lagging behind.

The key to helping your shy child is giving him reasons to be more comfortable in social settings. This means helping him acquire social competence as he builds relationships. This is created through:

- The quality of the parents' relationship with each other.
- The conveyance of positive beliefs about the nature of children and childhood.
- Parental tolerance for and understanding of emotions, especially "negative ones" (e.g., anger, fear, sadness, anxiety).

Here are some practical ideas:

- Have him ask for a glass of water at a friend's house. Don't pave the road for him—he needs safe challenges to build off of. (We had our shy child go to the register by himself to pay for items in stores while we waited nearby. He balked a few times, then finally did it. After about five years of help with shyness, he ran for student body president—and won!)
- Allow him some dominion over his life. Allow him to make small decisions that affect his life (the décor of his room, choice of clothing). Don't roll your eyes at his answers.
- Give her some control over what she does in her spare time. Being too busy puts her out of connection with peers.
- Let her cut her own meat or other food when she's old enough.
- Don't make him your emotional pillow—it robs him of assertive energy and will.
- Help with gradual exposure to fearful situations. (When going to a new school or even back to the same one, walk the grounds with her during the summertime.)
- Don't overvalue compliance. Total compliance to adult demands discourages children from asserting themselves. Leave room for negotiation on some issues.
- Most shy kids overestimate the visibility of their discomfort. Help yours understand that most everyone feels awkward

from time to time. If he assumes other people can see his great discomfort, help him see that this is not necessarily so.

## DINNER TALK

Dinnertime is special in our home, the most stimulating part of our everyday family life. A recent Census Bureau report reminds us how important this ritual is in the life of families across the board. It found that 79 percent of children five and younger, 73 percent of children six to eleven, and 58 percent of children twelve to seventeen had dinner with their parents every day during a typical week. "Family meals are still the norm in the American family," says Brett Brown, a researcher at Child Trends Inc., which recently issued a paper on the importance of eating together. Teens who eat regularly with their families are more likely to do well in school, delay sexual activity, have better mental health, and are less likely to get into fights, think about suicide or smoke, drink, or use drugs. "For kids who are facing other challenges, this is actually a great strength, an asset."[10]

My wife, Sandy, is a fantastic cook and hospitable entertainer, so much so that she has her own blog for people who want to entertain but are reluctant to do so.[11] Her hosting skills draw everyone to the table, but more than that, it's when we really talk together. As we go around the table, each person tells how the day went (including our kids' guests). It's their time to share what's on their mind and to answer a few questions if they want to. This is how we stay connected, and it's usually lively, a time to let down our hair. Lots of laughs and jokes.

Some of our guests plainly aren't used to this amount of talking with their families. They're taken aback by it, especially by the volume of conversation (at times), which are unscripted. Our kids aren't told what to think or say; they can express their will and their feelings, even when they're off-base.

For example, when one of our children has been humiliated at school, we might hear about plots of revenge against the kids who did it. We allow our child's anger to come out. And then we reason with him. We help him act *upon* his anger instead of acting it out. We talk about how hurting kids hurt other kids. (This doesn't excuse bad behavior but helps put it into perspective.)

The name of one nemesis comes up over and over, the name of a very troubled child. We talk about paths of truth and plans of action: For instance, winners don't focus on revenge; this or that is the best way to handle the problem; until the situation changes, no amount of talking is going to change [that kid's] emotions; here's why that kid is prone to find provocation where there is none, and so on.

**ONE REASON WE'RE SO QUICK TO SHUT OUR CHILDREN DOWN IS THAT STRONG-ARMING THEM IS SO MUCH EASIER AND SO MUCH LESS "TIME-CONSUMING."**

In order to help them avoid the downside of shyness, our children are both seen *and* heard. They're allowed to express themselves, even when their emotions are exaggerated and negative. We help them handle their feelings instead of saying they shouldn't feel them. They learn during our conversations that they can come to us for solutions. We're strong enough to handle their problems (even when we reel in private!).

I'll be straightforward: Though this interaction is immensely enjoyable and worthwhile a million times over, it's also tiring, especially at the end of the workday, and especially when I'm under a deadline. Let's be honest, parents: One reason we're so quick to shut our children down is that strong-arming them is so much easier and so much less "time-consuming." Much easier than listening. Much easier than learning. Much easier than loving.

But we cannot afford not to listen to, learn from, and love our children. Whatever it takes for us to have the time and energy we need for raising them righteously, that's what we must do.

# HELICOPTER MOMS, MOMMA BEARS, AND GRIZZLY MOMS

As previously mentioned, maternal overprotection is lethal to boys and young men. As a coach I've seen a lot of this, so I want to give a glimpse into our minds—how we view such mothers, what this means for their young men, and how to avoid damaging a son with good intentions.

I teach boys, young men, and sometimes young women how to play soccer. After more than a decade of coaching, I can't remember receiving disdainful and contemptuous words from one father. This doesn't mean there haven't been disagreements. It means most guys know how to treat another guy, something most of us learned on the playgrounds of our youth. Most guys know how to leave another man with his dignity intact.

Comparing my experiences with mothers to my experiences with fathers is remarkable. I've had fathers express concern about their kid's playing time or treatment from other players. But the way they do it doesn't make their son appear weak or needy in the eyes of everyone else. And they are civil—they stay in the realm of concern without crossing over into the swamp of overprotection.

Not so for what coaches call "Helicopter Moms," who hover above their children in a near-constant state of anxiety; "Momma Bears," those who are highly protective of their children and don't care if they disparage others in the process; and "Grizzly Moms," a highly dangerous breed who seem unwilling to stop at anything in getting their child what they want.

*Helicopter Moms* come with every season. In most cases, most of the time, they are helpful. Their sons usually do well in sports, though these boys sometimes lack a vital male energy (the ancient Greeks called it *thumos*—a tenacious, pugnacious, and animating spiritedness found more in men than women). I see these mothers asking their sons a lot of questions, and I see the boys trying to be kind in return, but also resenting such persistent doting and worry. The moms' frenzied over-involvement seems to drain their sons of confidence and courage, two powerful benefits of *thumos*.

I've also noticed that Helicopter Moms either don't have husbands or don't have husbands who show up for their son's games. These mothers are trying to be both parents, and I admire them for this. I can see how it hurts them when their sons try to push them away so they can enter and take part in the world of men.

*Momma Bears* have claws and use them, often behind the scenes. They verbally sucker-punch. They intend to ambush, to put me on my heels. They often begin with a false and misleading statement about me and then ask me to defend myself.

That's an old ploy that I don't bite on anymore. Without exception, Momma Bears have an inflated view of their child's abilities, a view he sometimes adopts. You can tell after a while: These players tend to parrot words and ideas that aren't common to their age. When they fail to dominate in a game like they've said they can, like their parents *know* they can, they say it wasn't their doing—other players let them down or deliberately excluded them from the game's normal flow. They believe they are being persecuted unfairly. A belief, I think, that comes directly from command central: Momma Bear's mouth.

Momma Bears, of course, in no way represent all soccer

moms. I've had great conversations with moms who disagree with me. But their approach is different. They aren't out for a pound of my flesh, and they aren't out to take all the bumps and bruises out of their kid's life. More times than not, they want clarification and better communication.

The son of a Momma Bear deflates when she's around. He looks at the ground. He lacks confidence. Whatever power he possessed before she showed up is gone, seeped into the patches of grass under his feet.

I have never punished a cub of a Momma Bear. I also don't retaliate at players because of their parents, though I know coaches who do. Here's something Momma Bears should know: Coaches talk. We warn each other about you, like signs in a campground revealing the presence of dangerous animals.

Sometimes your child won't make a team because of you. For example, if he's a "bubble" player—meaning a coach could go either way in keeping or cutting a player from a roster—and if he has a Momma Bear behind him, he is most likely cut. Most coaches are volunteers. Why should they keep your kid and put up with you?

Cubs end up paying in other ways too. Because coaches are forced to walk on eggshells around Momma Bears, they often, sometimes unknowingly, marginalize their kids during practice so as to avoid any further contact with Mom. Or a coach with less backbone will over-favor the kid and give him more playing time than his skills should allow. His teammates notice, and this can set into motion a level of disdain the coach might not even sense, much less do anything about. The cub is losing friends through no fault of his own. It's an ugly situation all the way around.

When I get an overprotected cub, my usual tasks are either (1) helping him see that he's not as good as he (and she) thinks he is, or more commonly, (2) helping him see that's he's better than he currently realizes. Often my endeavor is to help him trust himself. I help him believe in himself by telling and showing him that I believe in him.

*Grizzly Moms* are unstoppable, rage-filled, even delusional. A Grizzly Mom will demand anything, no matter how farfetched, to give her son the advantages presumed to be his birthright. The only words that appease her are "Yes, ma'am," and the only words that put her on her heels are "restraining order." I have yet to see one show affection to her husband, who is usually in the background minding his manners, hoping to stay out of the way. Healthy women stay clear of Grizzly Moms, and they pity their sons.

One season I had numerous players tell me they were going to quit the team if a certain boy was allowed to stay on it. I saw what he did during practice and games, and it would take your breath away. His mouth was filthy; he said some of the cruelest things I've ever heard. Sometimes other parents were in tears over what he said.

I called his home to tell the family of my decision to remove him. Unfortunately, his mom answered, and I quickly figured out the origin of his attitude. I would never accept that kind of abuse now, but then I thought I was obligated to hear her out. Her profane, hateful words flew screaming into my ear; I had to hold the phone away.

She wouldn't listen to reason. When I told her that if we lost all the players ready to leave, there wouldn't be enough to play a legal game, she told me to contact the league and demand an exception. (Every Momma Bear and Grizzly Mom requires special rules and privileges for her son, whether or not it tramples other kids in the process.) I hung up after repeatedly trying to speak with her. She was still yelling.

If a father spoke this way to a female coach, he'd be tarred and feathered in the court of public opinion. As it stands today, Grizzly Moms get a free pass. There is no social pressure that keeps them at bay, which would also rescue their children from psychological fragility that will continue to hobble their development.

Grizzly Mom behavior on the sidelines is the stuff of legends. It's so bad that it's often used as comedic fodder, even though it isn't funny. There are at least three groups that experience tremendous turnover due to unrestrained abuse: Good teachers, nurses, and coaches often leave their vital social-wellness forums in order to escape their teeth and claws.

There are so many sad components to overprotection of children. It's a dynamic no sane parent intends to begin, but when it does, it continues, and the results can hinder children well into adulthood, *if* indeed they ever do grow up. Any way you cut *this* parenting pie, everyone loses. "The joy of parenting" is a haunting phrase with no personal application for moms and dads. Kids either become arrogant or passive. Neither parent nor child wins.

There's one group of kids who get overlooked when we consider the dangerous practice of overprotection: kids who really need more adult help and more peer support, kids who are disadvantaged physically, mentally, economically, and socially. They receive less help because too many parents are over-obsessing on too few kids and neglecting our society's most needy. The weakest in our midst need those with abundance to share their abundance. We cannot continue to ignore our growing inability to care about, and for, one another.

These children have been receiving a perplexing bushel of mixed relational messages and unfulfilled expectations of love, respect, and healthy support. Our culture is receiving countless underdeveloped souls too broken and me-centered to muster the ability to exercise moral courage on behalf of justice for all. We need to start preparing fresh graduating classes.

CHAPTER

5

# THE LINE BETWEEN PROTECTION AND OVERPROTECTION

Ninety percent of adults believe the world is more dangerous today than when they grew up. Is the majority right? After a quick review of the good ol' days, I'm not so sure.

The good ol' days were when kids died in car wrecks with seat belts dangling around their ankles instead of snug across their lap and chest. (And air bags were science fiction.) Overall, fatal vehicle accidents have dropped 25 percent since 1960, and a child's chance of dying due to an accident is down a whopping 50 percent during the same period.

In the good ol' days, many kids were exposed to volcano-like plumes of secondhand smoke. Death by cancer is down 30 percent since 1960.

Recall that in the good ol' days my father carried his baby sister's body to the cemetery after she died of dehydration from a common ailment that's now routinely treated. Have you known any child who died from dehydration?

The good ol' days saw parents battering their children and calling it discipline. When they screamed at their children so loudly the neighbors heard, few intervened; they were uncomfortable, but they didn't call the police to offer testimony. (It wasn't until the release of the article "The Battered Child Syndrome" in 1962 that child abuse came to the forefront of our culture's [very reluctant] thinking.)

The good ol' days permitted teachers to beat down a child with both hands and words; sometimes that kid went home to receive an additional beating.

In the good ol' days, most kids were seen, not heard. Many fathers thought it was women's work to rear children, resulting in a father hunger that still gnaws at lives today, especially among juvenile delinquents and adult inmates. Parents told daughters that college wasn't an option for them, and they didn't need it anyway, since they were girls. Dialing 9-1-1 got you nowhere. And there was no Poison Control Hotline.

Also, two of the world's good-ol'-days superpowers had the capacity (but thankfully not the will) to blow up the planet; to be "ready" for a nuclear attack, students practiced air-raid drills by crawling under their desks.

Furthermore, let's not forget that in the good ol' days, those who suffered from depression and other mental illnesses were likely candidates to be institutionalized; most of them, and those who loved them, lived without help from counseling or medication.

Are kids really in more danger now than before? We think they must be when we consider atrocities like the 1999 shootings at Columbine High School and say, "This must be proof that it's never been worse." But we need to do our homework. For example, in 1927, more than seven decades earlier, in Bath Township, Michigan, school-board member Andrew Kehoe, through a series of bombings, killed forty-five people and injured fifty-eight. The Bath School Disaster claimed three times as many lives as Columbine, and most were children between the second and sixth grades. It remains the deadliest act of mass murder at a school in U.S. history.

No wonder the writer of Ecclesiastes warns us to not look upon the past with fondness.

I'm not trying to put down the past or paint it black. I have my fondness for parts of it as well—for one thing, I feel that good-ol'-days neighborliness and hospitality have slipped markedly and that we'd do well to rediscover it.

Clearly, in some ways we're far better off. And without question, in some ways we're not—a shocking increase of weapons in school and teenage suicide being two of the most outstanding examples. It's safe to say that when it comes to well-being, every generation can rightly claim to have made some steps forward and some steps back.

My critique is only an attempt to put our lives in a broader framework. That's the main purpose of this chapter, and the next is putting our parenting role in perspective by figuring out what our kids should and shouldn't be cautious of, both inside and out-

**IN MANY WAYS, WHAT HAPPENS TO KIDS AT HOME IS FAR MORE LIKELY TO ENHANCE OR DESTROY THEIR SAFETY THAN WHAT HAPPENS ELSEWHERE.**

side their home. In many ways, what happens to them at home is far more likely to enhance or destroy their safety than what happens elsewhere. Or as former First Lady Barbara Bush put it, what happens inside our house is far more important than what happens inside the White House.

Our work of discernment requires pushing past persistent myths and into unchanging truths. There are unintended negative consequences to always trying to keep everything on "the safe side," which in some ways is actually the harmful side. We want to learn the difference between smart protection and damaging overprotection. Between being wise and being naïve. Between choosing intelligently and succumbing to fear.

Before we dive in, I want you to consider one factor: There is a "spirit of the age" in this world that wants us to get this important work wrong. It wants us befuddled and misdirected. It's an evil influence, as C. S. Lewis observed, that wants us to think the bow of our parenting boat is on fire, when all the while it's the stern. It wants us to think we're being good parents as we rush to fight on a popular front . . . so it can attack us from the rear, where we aren't looking. It's an insidious enticement to bite at easy answers that bring us short-term emotional comfort but no actual knowledge that will truly protect our children from harm.

It's a mindset that, for example, has us thinking it's the creepy-looking man in the trench coat who's most likely to sexually abuse our daughters, when the facts have told us for decades that a perpetrator is far more likely to be a clean-shaven and "nice" male relative. In pondering this deceptive spirit, instead of kicking at the darkness, let's create some light instead, knowing, or at least considering, that there is a force opposing our good desire to love and safeguard our kids. Parenting is best done by the wise and the shrewd.

## "NOTHING EDUCATIONAL OR WORTH SEEING"

Child safety advocate Gavin DeBecker has a clever acronym for "news": Nothing Educational or Worth Seeing. Treating television news like the R-rated material it is, he keeps a lid on it with his children. DeBecker is far from naïve about the world, and, given his extensive work in the realm of child safety, my guess is his kids are better prepared for life than many, if not most. He's not trying to keep his kids from knowing about darkness. To the contrary, he's trying to keep their perception sharp and keen; he keeps television highly restricted because television, by its nature, distorts perception. (Often not deliberate, but nevertheless true.) TV news presents concentrated ugliness, strife, wickedness, and evil as the predominant mainstream of what's actually happening. A consistent diet of it produces a sensationalized, imbalanced sense of what's going on around us.

Some parents want their young children to watch "the news," thinking it will help them understand the "real world." Two main problems with this approach: (1) It doesn't come close to presenting the "real world" to most anyone, and (2) it may well plant overarching fear into your child, creating the very kind of boy or girl that becomes a victim in the hands of adult predators and peer bullies.

When I ask on my talk show, "Have you seen a shooting in real life?" the only people who say yes are soldiers and police officers. No civilian has yet to say yes, and very, very few have witnessed any such thing. Yet violent, person-to-person gunfire events are teleported into our homes almost every time we turn on the news. Disconnecting the TVs, or using them selectively, may be the most valuable and effective home security system you can install.

There is most likely no greater creator of warped perception (next to illicit drug use) than television; turning it off is psychological protection for our kids. If you let it, television will show them an unending reel of abductions, murders, exploitations, assaults, shootings, and bodies being wheeled out of homes. One person's ordeal becomes everybody's brush with evil; as time passes, the child watching can come to feel he or she has personally experienced thousands of journeys into darkness, and with the trauma, whether perceived or not, comes victim-creating timidity and fearfulness.

Dr. Katherine Ramsland, professor of forensic psychology, told me:

> An overemphasis on fearsome things that *might* happen encourages children to become timid and restricted in their awareness. They withdraw from the richness of life and fail to develop self-confidence from testing their personal resources. Such children have a certain look that transmits a sense of vulnerability and a lack of self-assurance. Predators quickly learn that children without confidence or inner resources are often compliant, trusting, and unable to resist. They'll also be easily intimidated into keeping the molester's secret. Parents who overprotect children or make them afraid of the outside world inhibit them from acquiring confidence in their own abilities as they mature and test themselves.

Sandy and I did an experiment. For an entire month we unplugged all electronic media in our home for our kids and ourselves. No one could use a computer (except for work or homework). No computer games, and no television unless we watched it together, usually no more than one hour. When we did watch, we chose shows like *America's Funniest Home Videos, MythBusters, Dirty Jobs,* and *Good Eats.*

As you can imagine, there was a backlash at first, though it didn't last as long as we expected. We were all far more civil to each other even after just a few days. Then, gradually, we were far more caring about each other. We played games. We swam. Kicked a soccer ball around. Read books. We did more family activities, like going for walks and even grooming our dog for a change (he finally looked like someone loves him). We had more fun together than we'd had in a long time. Everyone was more peaceful, and we showed each other more grace. It was obvious how much electronic entertainment had been coming between us.

Most experts agree: Restrict access to television (some say throw it away), and not just news, but everything that makes murder and gore and horror look commonplace. TV violence has a disproportionate effect on aggressive children, and poor academic performance is also highly linked to the consumption of television violence. Those who fail in school watch more TV, which isolates them from their peers and gives them less time to work for academic success. The cycle of aggression, academic failure, social failure, and violence-viewing can be so tightly bound that it tragically perpetuates itself.

## INCLINATION AND INTUITION

It's a loaded word, *intuition*. This is at least partly because so many of us mistake intuition for our own *inclination*. Inclination primarily describes "a feeling that pushes somebody to make a particular choice or decision."[1] Intuition is "the state of being aware of or knowing something without having to discover or perceive it, or the ability to do this."[2]

In preferring inclination over intuition, we're often prone to forgo discernment and guidance (intuition) in favor of our default perspective and already established biases (inclination). Intuition, though, can be a powerful compass reading that helps us find the sand-covered line we seek (between protection and overprotection). Intuition can mean going with your gut sense in a way that helps you cut through the fog and choose wisely, even if you're not sure why that insight occurred. Intuition, sometimes, is clarity for unclear reasons.

Child safety experts agree that parents not only need to listen to intuition, they also need to sharpen it and remove obstacles in front of it. Obstacles such as the belief that parents and children must always be polite even in a dangerous situation, or the idea that only "shady-looking" people abuse kids. When the path for intuition is cleared, it's a brilliant guide for parents who want to steer their children away from harm.

In some cases, however, parents of victims and parents of perpetrators don't just reject intuition and stick with inclination; sometimes they are unwilling (and perhaps, to a degree, unable) to see and acknowledge what's right in front of them. Consider, for example, twenty-five-year-old Kimveer Gill, who on September 13, 2006, arrived at Dawson College in Montreal and opened fire on students within the main building, killing eighteen-year-old Anastasia De Sousa and wounding nineteen others. When police officers shot him in the arm, Gill turned his gun on himself and committed suicide. His actions were premeditated, and a short suicide note was found on his body during the autopsy.

Gill had been declared unsuitable for military service and lived in his parents' basement. Apparently his most intimate relationship was with the Internet, where he spewed violence and conceit, claimed he "feared nothing," alleged that "cops are corrupt sons of whores," raged in furious hatred against God's people, and declared that nearly everyone and everything is worthless. He announced that he wanted to die "in a hail of gunfire."

Describing himself, he wrote:

His name is Trench. You will come to know him as the Angel of Death. . . . He is not a people person. He has met a handfull [sic] of people in his life who are decent. But he finds the vast majority to be worthless, no good, kniving [sic], betraying, lieing [sic], deceptive, motherfu—. . . . Work sucks . . . school sucks . . . life sucks . . . what else can I say? . . . Life is a video game you've got to die sometime. . . .

I am locked in an invisible cage within my head. There

is no chance of escape. . . . The police are watching me. They actually think I don't know this. They are monitering [sic] my movements. Hey pigs. . . . You shouldn't be pretending to be nice little goth girls, and doing surveilance [sic] on people. . . .

I pledge Allegiance to Marilyn Manson; I pledge Allegiance to Goth; I pledge Allegiance to Anarchy; I pledge Allegiance to Black Metal. . . .

F—— THE WORLD. You're all animals. I can see through you. When I look in your eyes I can see your thoughts. You're nothing at all. Just animals.

All of this had been taking place within the family home, and this young man had lived a quarter century. His disposition and his moods were foul, black, foreboding, ominous. So how did Kimveer Gill's mother describe him after being told about his evil rampage upon students with whom he had no connection? He was a "good boy." She had no idea what was going on, "no idea that her son was harboring such dark thoughts." She said, "If I knew a little bit that recently his mind is changing to other directions, we would have done something."[3]

Whether or not law enforcement was actually watching, his mother noticed nothing. (Other parents of murderers have responded similarly.) I'm pointing this out because sometimes "mother's intuition" is a feel-good notion that in its extreme is dangerous. Intuition *would* have tipped off Gill's mom. Her inclination, though, was to overlook what was taking place.

Let's be clear. Healthy people have healthy intuition. If a parent's mind is deluged by forces or motives that skew her understanding, then her intuition isn't going to function clearly. We can't get clean water from contaminated wells. Once a parent is in a place of not being able to rely on intuition, encouraging her to follow her intuition will probably send her further in the wrong direction, further from the perspective we really need as parents.

And when we're unable or unwilling to see the truth, fear is often a primary culprit.

## WHEN FEAR DRIVES LIVES

My first book took on conspiracy theories: why some people believe in them and why some are even willing to die for them. I debated numerous theorists across the country and was interviewed by C-SPAN and the *New York Times,* among many other media outlets. The conspiracy theorists had read the same news reports I'd read about national and international affairs, but we interpreted them very differently.

My best attempts to talk them down from that ledge of life did hardly any good. The theorists *had* to believe in their theories, even when I was able to show them how contradictory they themselves were and how blatantly absurd were the alleged conspiracies. Conspiracy theories are a kind of security blanket woven together to help the theorist make sense of the world. Such people were transmitters, not receivers, of information—they couldn't receive new or objective information because they'd already decided where everything would fit into their already established labyrinth of self-protection.

Remember that conspiracy theories don't just consume individuals (think of Waco, Ruby Ridge, Oklahoma City). The resultant actions by those who are consumed hurt us all, and most notably their spouses and kids; I received numerous letters from wives and children of theorists (most are men), begging for help. A conspiracy theorist's fearful view of the world always hurts those who love him but cannot reach him; he refuses to set aside or reject any of his inclinations in order to begin relying on intuition.

This is similar to what can happen with parents who overprotect—many of them have so deeply entrenched their worried habits and perspectives into their families that they don't relate to their kids intuitively. Increasingly frenzied by life's pace and by their own anxiety, their mental and emotional inclinations begin to rule their children in ways that eventually result in kids simply shutting down. As we've already noted, this is happening in younger and younger kids. Children of all ages are becoming less and less able to function, and while we'd like to think it's because the world has become so dark, or because society has become so generally misguided, it's usually because the problem is rooted, fostered, and festering at home.

Most overprotective parents don't use clean intuition; the real problem, frequently, is that they think they're using it. But true intuition leads to good results. Overarching fear, the driving force of worry, doesn't, even when it's couched in ways that in the short term appear good and noble to other overprotective parents. *When we're convinced that life is a tragedy waiting to happen, our kids suffer.*

I remember when what I called intuition backfired. I'd hired three men to move my hot tub, and when they pulled up and jumped out of their truck, they looked to me as though they may well have just

## WHEN WE'RE CONVINCED THAT LIFE IS A TRAGEDY WAITING TO HAPPEN, OUR KIDS SUFFER.

been released from prison. My daughter, uncharacteristically, went to open the door.

My blood roared inside. A primal sap flowed from my gut, throughout my body. My inner-protector (I call him Thor, God of Thunder) drew his sword. I yelled, "Don't open the door!" She escaped to her room.

I helped them move the tub, a beast of a job involving nearly six hours of difficult labor. I don't claim to have gotten to know them. I enjoyed working alongside them, and while I made sure they didn't enter my home, none of them gave me the willies.

What flared up inside me when they arrived wasn't intuition. It was inclination via stereotypes that threw all kinds of warning bells in my head, and I sounded the alarm loudly in my home. Not at all to say I shouldn't have had any thought to safeguard my family while they worked on my property. But so what if none of them owns a pair of Dockers? Knowing what I know now about which kids get abused and by whom (90 percent of sexual abuse committed by a man is done by someone the child knows, not a stranger), I would be more productive observing relatives at family functions than worrying about hot tub movers.

If you suspect you need your intuition adjusted, clear the way for honesty so you can find out to what level fear, rather than intuition, is driving your decisions with your kids. Remember this helpful acronym for FEAR: *False Evidence Appearing Real.* All fear is not false; fear that's justifiable can be extremely helpful. But false fear can lead to unhealthy anger and blurred perception.

Ask friends if they think you're overprotective of your children. Ask a certain kind of friend, someone you know is willing to be truthful, even if it means he or she makes you uncomfortable at times. Ask someone whose perception you admire and who isn't prone to gossip or excessively harsh criticism.

Tell them they're free to tell you the truth, even if it hurts, and that you won't punish them afterward. (Giving this green light to key people in my life has kept me from making some awful decisions.) Then, truly listen, and don't correct. Do not completely deny their claim. Instead, ask for clarification and, if possible, examples. Cry if you need to, then act on the information you've been given. This is how wise parents can fine-tune their intuition.

In addition to asking friends, you might consider making an appointment with a counselor.

## GET YOURSELF UNDER CONTROL

Fearful children often come from fearful parents whose intuition is skewed and whose inclination is over-empowered. Furthermore, fearful people are often angry people in disguise and/or denial. This anger can become a wicked force in a child's life, and the consequences are tremendous; it's critical that parents with an angry disposition get themselves under control.

Contrary to common perception, mothers are more likely to physically abuse and even murder their children than fathers. Child abuse perpetrators are 62.3% female; child fatality perpetrators are 62.8% female.[4] The mother/father ratio is actually greater because many of the male abusers counted aren't biological fathers but stepfathers or boyfriends. Regarding murders of children by single parents, the estimated total in the report is 264 parental murders of children committed by single custodial mothers and eleven by single custodial fathers.[5] There are roughly five times as many single custodial mothers as single custodial fathers; the child-murder ratio, though, is twenty-five to one.[6]

I come from abuse. I know what it does to a kid. If you abuse, and if you want to darken your child's future and fill him with psychological "holes," keep pretending that everything's great and that it's everyone else's fault that you're out of control.

One of the most insidious psychological holes: Children of abuse are not only less likely to stand up to abuse by others, they do not stand up "for themselves to themselves," explains Hara Estroff Marano.[7] They not only believe bad things said about them by others, they do not even denounce their own self-attacks, such as "I'm so stupid," or "It's my fault people beat me up," or "Whatever I do doesn't matter," or "I'm worthless!" and so on. As I explain in *No More Christian Nice Guy*, children of abuse become their own worst enemies by bearing false witness— against themselves.

If you are fearful, angry, or abusive, and if you don't care if your children suffer abuse from others later in life and have their own intuition distorted, keep justifying your behavior. Keep playing the blame game. Keep attacking the rare person who shows enough courage to confront you. Keep assassinating the character of those who possess more character than you do.

Abusers know that with enough force, deceit, and manipulation they can keep entire family trees at bay. Nevertheless, if you are angry and abusive, the kind of parent who creates victims of abuse, you're not fooling anyone. In time your tyranny will be exposed for what it really is. After all, you are raising your own biographers. Rejecting humility and pressing forward in pride may result in their turning their back on you. In your later years you may howl in protest if no one is there to ease your pain, but you will have brought it on yourself.

If you abuse your children, take an honest look at your upbringing. Like my mother, you'll most likely see that you are doing to others what was done to you. You didn't deserve that abuse. But neither do your children.

Break the chain that binds your lineage. I did, and so have many others. Gather people around you who will help you overcome this problem. There will be shame and guilt to handle. Feel them—experience them, because they are required for healthy change—then move on. Don't stay stuck in remorse forever. The goal isn't to eternally serve penance but to begin learning how to live by loving.

Ongoing, seemingly never-ending sorrow is sometimes an excuse to avoid the next phase, which is changing how you respond to stress and fear. Your kids don't want you to be continually broken in this way, and neither does God. Both need you to rise up and to start using your parental strength justly.

## IF YOU'RE DEPRESSED, SEEK TREATMENT

Moms are far more likely to be diagnosed with depression than dads. Parental, especially maternal, depression has a devastating effect on kids. It essentially removes a parent from the life of a child, and everything can seem unclear to the child since the parent is physically present but emotionally unavailable. Depression erodes a parent's ability to respond positively to a child. Maternal depression is such a powerful negative force in the life of children that, all by itself—even without the anger and rage that often accompanies it—it creates numerous problems for them in relating to the outside world. Depression not only limits a parent's availability to her child, it increases parental irritability and leads to the use of coercive tactics. Depression, like worry, distorts the keen perception we need to find the line between protection and overprotection.

According to the U.S. National Institute of Mental Health (NIMH), the main symptoms and signs of depression are:

- ▶ Persistent sad, anxious, or "empty" mood
- ▶ Feelings of hopelessness, pessimism
- ▶ Feelings of guilt, worthlessness, helplessness
- ▶ Loss of interest or pleasure in hobbies and activities that were once enjoyed, including sex
- ▶ Decreased energy, fatigue, being "slowed down"
- ▶ Difficulty concentrating, remembering, making decisions
- ▶ Insomnia, early-morning awakening, or oversleeping
- ▶ Appetite and/or weight loss, or overeating and weight gain
- ▶ Thoughts of death or suicide; suicide attempts
- ▶ Restlessness, irritability

▶ Persistent physical symptoms that do not respond to treatment, such as headaches, digestive disorders, and chronic pain

If you've been experiencing several of these symptoms to a degree that they've affected or impaired your life, talk to your doctor, who can help you find out whether you're suffering from depression and then direct you to appropriate resources for treatment and recovery.

## EXERCISE AND PRAY

Related to getting yourself under control is the need for exercise. Studies continue to show that regular exercise can be as effective as some medications in treating depression. And of course exercise is helpful not only to the depressed, but to everyone.

The regular exercise my wife and I undertake helps keep us sane and gives us energy, and it also makes us more relaxed and focused as parents. Sandy has cultivated numerous running partners, which helps her keep her routine. The hardest part of a workout *is* getting out the door; exercise partners help you get out the door. And I've never regretted a good workout.

Exercise programs and magazines do us a great disservice when they put the culture's gods and goddesses on the cover. Don't be misled. Regular exercise is not a huge commitment. Three days a week, half an hour at a time, can make a big difference in the life of a parent who wants to protect her child without going overboard.

One piece of hard-won advice (I played competitive soccer for eighteen years and also raced bicycles): Do yourself a favor and start out slow. Don't let initial enthusiasm get the best of you, because you may end up so sore you won't want to get out of bed.

At the beginning, enthusiasm is too important to misspend, because the benefits of exercise are not as apparent right away as they will be within a week or two. You'll need to push through that initial phase, and you may not feel the increased energy at first. So use common sense. If you're starting from scratch, for instance, walk around the block for a few days and then stretch afterward; incrementally, you can tackle something larger.

Prayer also goes hand in hand with getting yourself under control. I believe that sincere prayers for help and guidance—even when not completely focused—accomplish something. If you're a person who thinks you need to get your act together before you can communicate with God, read the parable of the prodigal son (Luke 15). You'll see that the younger, wayward son does not show true repentance when he turns home toward his father, who, in the parable, represents God the Father. He doesn't have his act together; he's seeking help and refuge more than forgiveness. Yet Jesus tells us that God comes running down the road to those who ask for help and that He celebrates their return to Him. He is not the Great Ogre in the Sky. He is our exuberant and extravagant Father.

In your prayer time, find specific reasons for gratefulness. Start with your own body—the fact that you have clothing to wear. Shoes are a sign of blessing in many countries; we often have enough to consider them clutter. Express gratefulness for the health you have. And so on.

A wise friend of mine, Mike Smith, co-founder of GodMen (*www.godmen.com*), told me that he studied the qualities shared by successful people. At the top of the list was gratefulness. This doesn't mean they didn't have problems. It means their gratefulness helped them transcend their problems.

Finally, make better eating and sleeping habits your priorities.

One very common mistake is consuming too many simple carbohydrates, which create weight gain and don't provide sustained energy. Also, most people with sleep problems don't rest enough before they go to bed to ensure quality sleep; they also tend to drink or ingest too many stimulants.

See the common denominator in all these suggestions? *Honing your perception (wisdom) and building up your energy (strength).* You need both in order to provide healthy protection for others. Those who depend upon you need your donations of keen insight and consistent strength, which, in the parental context, are donations of love.

## HOW HEALTHY ARE YOUR BOUNDARIES?

In order to find the line between protection and overprotection, we need to take an honest look at our own understanding of who we are and how we relate to others. Specifically, we need to discover if we are too passive or too aggressive with others; one way or the other, our children are likely to inherit or incorporate much of what we display. If we show them an assertive approach toward life, they will be leagues ahead in knowing how to ward off anyone who would seek to take advantage of them.

Passive people react, or underreact, to life's issues instead of being proactive; they may or may not respond, but either way they do not initiate. Aggressive people overreact to what's happening around them. The passive and the aggressive alike are usually motivated by fear.

Fear—fear of disapproval or of conflict—causes the passive person to acquiesce and the aggressive person to attack. Passive people create soft boundaries, easily penetrated by abusers who use their weakness against them. Aggressive people erect boundaries so rigid that they can't be reached; they expect so much conflict, and are so busy creating it, that they see provocation where none is to be found. Both passive and aggressive people isolate themselves from others, even people who have nothing but warm regard for them.

Assertive people, on the other hand, are proactive, which helps them create the right boundaries for themselves and for those in their charge. They respond with the right amount of power *and* grace. They don't hurt people unnecessarily, but they do get their point across. They have an air that acts as a repellant to would-be abusers.

The assertive don't have the disease to please others like the passive, who let other people take advantage because they fear disapproval or criticism if they were to erect a healthy boundary. The assertive also don't senselessly bludgeon others like the aggressive, who fear that conflict or embarrassment might come from anyone getting too close. The boundaries of the assertive are both strong and permeable—yet permeable only to those deemed fit to have intimate access.

Assertive people build good fences between them and others, and though they're no one's fool, they are not cold, distant, or cut off from others. Their personality creates many gates, but only to the right kind of people. They're comfortable in their own skin, so they don't feel the need to try to control others, and they're not controlled by others. Most everyone, except the abuser, likes the assertive. They're not mastered by fear, anxiety, or worry, so their perception of life and their intuition are clearer than most. That's where we want to be as parents.

Here's the thing: *Whether or not we as parents are interested in conflict, conflict is interested in us and our children.* Take a mental scan of your social boundaries. Do you cave in too easily to demands, letting others come into your life too easily, making you uncomfortable and resentful? This is what I once did, more than I care to admit. This is how passive people live, and if you're familiar with my previous writing you'll know this is surviving, not thriving.

It's time to become more assertive. The passive make poor protectors of children because their borders don't hold much back. Time to build some fences with gates that let people in based on *your* criteria, not their desires.

Do you feel you have to beat people to the punch all the time or they'll punch you? Do you end up making friends but losing them quickly for reasons no one shares—it just happens? Do you ward off closeness with virtually everyone, even those of good-will? These are signs that you're too aggressive—if people wanted to be beat up all the time, they'd take up boxing instead of hanging around you.

It's time to become more assertive. The aggressive don't rightly protect children because their borders are impenetrable—they tend to lock their children away from the world. Time to start including gates in your fences so that when your children move more and more into life on their own, they will be neither painfully awkward nor wildly inappropriate, and most important, they will be a non-target for predators.

# SPOTTING AND REPELLING ADULT PREDATORS

Nice people may not be interested in the defiled world of predators, but predators are interested in their children. Adult predators, sexual or otherwise, aim to separate children from their parents and/or from other adults who might stop them. Most kids are not separated at gunpoint or knifepoint; rather they are lured away by those who earn trust in dishonest ways.

Here's how they earn our trust. (Gavin De Becker broadly calls these "Survival Signals.")

**Forced Teaming:** A predator uses the word *we* when *we* isn't true or accurate. It establishes premature trust and makes a kid feel obligated to stay around this adult. He says things like, "We're sure in a mess, aren't we?" Teach your child to say to a stranger, or to someone they know but do not trust, "I didn't ask for your help, and I don't want it. Leave me alone." This isn't wrong. It's wise.

**Charm and Niceness:** In order to deceive, you have to remain at least one step ahead of someone. Charm and niceness can hide intent and give a head start. People who take control of others almost always pretend to be nice in the beginning. Teach your children that "nice" is not the same as good. This is especially important for girls, who are generally expected to be warm and friendly toward adults.

**Too Many Details:** Con artists often use too many details to sell the story because they know that since it's not true, the story must be sold. After a while, details can wear down a person's defenses, as dishonest salespeople know well. Teach your child to consider context by asking herself, *Why is this person talking to me in the first place, and why is he telling me so many things?*

**Typecasting:** This involves a slight insult, usually one that's easy to refute. "You're one of those kids who's too scared to disagree with your parents, aren't you?" It's designed to get a child on the defensive, breaking down resistance. Teach your child he does not have to answer every question put to him. In some cases, short answers like "Whatever" are appropriate.

**Loan-Sharking:** Predators will often give a child something (the common example is candy) to make her feel indebted. It can also be advice or sympathy: "Your parents don't listen to you, do they? I'm glad to listen. I care about you even when others don't." Teach your kids not to accept gifts from people who want something in return. Otherwise it's not a gift—it's a debt installment.

**The Unsolicited Promise:** Someone promises to do something for a child who never asked for it but is getting it anyway. "Don't worry, I'll take care of you." Promises are used to convince us of an intention, but they are not guarantees. Nor does such a person behave in a way that he will guarantee anything. If he did, it would expose his deceitful intent. When someone provides an unsolicited promise, teach your child to think, *You're right. I am hesitant to trust you. Thank you for making that clear.*

**Discounting *No*:** Anyone who chooses not to hear the word *no* is trying to control your child. A frequent (and potentially dangerous) response in this situation is negotiation: "I really appreciate your offer, but let me try to do it on my own first." Teach your child, instead, to say out loud what she's really thinking. If that's "Bug off," she should say it. Teach her to look a person in the eyes with strength, to walk away, and to be loud if necessary. De Becker says, "You cannot turn a decent man into a violent one by being momentarily rude, but you can present yourself as an ideal target by appearing too timid"[1] (and nice).

# TALKING TO STRANGERS

If your child never talked to strangers, then he would never talk to a police officer or a store clerk. Telling a kid that strangers are dangerous equates strangers with danger, which prevents kids from finding that line between protection and

**IF YOUR CHILD NEVER TALKED TO STRANGERS, THEN HE WOULD NEVER TALK TO A POLICE OFFICER OR A STORE CLERK.**

overprotection. Once again, most predatory behavior toward children involves someone they know; pinning danger on strangers is one of the best ways to destroy a child's perception of and intuition about true danger. Instead, teach your children to evaluate behavior, specifically *strangeness* (not necessarily strangers). Teach them to pay attention to stares that last too long, a smile that's not real, rapid looking away, and other signs of discomfort.

If a stranger talks to you and your child and doesn't give off warning signs, talk with your child about why you felt safe around that man, and also what would have made you feel unsafe around him.

## WHEN IN DOUBT, GO TO A WOMAN

If your kid is lost in public, train him to ask a woman for help before asking a man. This does not contradict a fact mentioned

**Kids:** When you're away from home, make sure you know the full name of the hotel or motel where you're staying in case you get separated from your parents.

**Parents:** If possible, travel during daylight hours.

**Kids:** Don't wander away from the group. Stay alert and keep up.

**Parents:** Make sure there are enough adults to supervise children at an amusement park or museum; it's easier to get separated in large crowds.

**Kids:** Make sure you know your parents' full names and cell phone numbers in case you get separated from them on a trip.

**Parents:** Teach kids your address, phone number, and how to dial 9-1-1 in case you get separated.

**Kids:** If you get separated from your parent or guardian, don't go looking by yourself. Try to find an adult in a uniform or at an information booth.

**Parents:** Designate a central meeting spot at a park or mall in case you and your kids are separated. Also, travel with recent photos of your children to show in case they are lost.

**Kids:** Don't answer the door without a parent or guardian's permission.

**Parents:** Inform relatives and friends where you'll be traveling and how long you'll be gone. If you're not expecting visitors, don't answer the hotel door without first calling the front desk.

**Kids:** Don't swim in or play around any body of water you're unfamiliar with before a trusted adult checks it out and tells you it's okay.

**Parents:** Make sure hotel pools are supervised and well-protected.[2]

earlier, that a mother is more likely than a father to physically abuse her child. This is not her kid, and, furthermore, it's highly unlikely that she's a sexual predator. According to De Becker, a woman is more likely to stay involved in a lost child's trouble until it's resolved; a man is more likely to let authorities handle the problem.

## IT'S OKAY TO BE "MEAN"

You read it right. Kids should know that it's okay to be "mean." In fact, being good sometimes requires you to be "mean" to others. "Mean" in this context means conflict, which isn't always mean. Children need our help understanding this, because they are wired to seek the approval of adults, even when adults don't deserve it. Predators bank on that.

This is hard for Christian parents to accept if they believe it's wrong to use verbal and physical force. But read just the first few chapters of Mark's gospel and tell me Jesus didn't believe in or enter into deliberate conflict. Saying that Jesus (and, by default, Christianity) denounces conflict is like saying Karl Marx was a capitalist.

When it comes to self-protection, conflict is good. It does not mean retaliation. It means telling your kid it's okay to rebuff an adult and even injure one if needed. It's okay to yell and to otherwise make a scene—teach your child to yell, if he or she is being grabbed, "This is not my father!" (or mother). That's likely to get a bystander to step in, since most assume a child is being escorted by a parent.

Regarding authority, a child's view toward it can be dangerous in two key areas. If he questions authority too much, he will be blackballed by adults, who will find him unnecessarily contentious, and his peers won't like him much either. But if the child is too trusting of all authority, he sets himself up to become a naïve victim.

# PROTECTION FROM SEXUAL ABUSE

When it comes to sexual abuse, keep the following truth in mind: Male family members can deliver your child and you from all kinds of harm, and they can deliver all kinds of harm as well.

No one who's familiar with my body of writing can say I'm anti-guy. I think men get a bad rap in society, and there is a profound prejudice against them in church. Men are regularly marginalized, lied about, and lampooned with very little outcry. But the body of evidence in this area is simply overwhelming. Heterosexual men commit the vast majority of sexual abuse in America, more than 90 percent.

Some say it's because of how all guys are wired. I contend that it's the result of the lack of fathering and, with it, the lack of male integrity. The prison population bears this out: Approximately 85 percent of male inmates grew up without fathers. Boys need men to show them how to be men and to help keep them from going over the cliffs of life.

## KIDS NEED TO KNOW WE'LL PROTECT THEM

De Becker says,

[My greatest contribution] to solving the mystery of aberrant behavior is my refusal to call it a mystery. Rather, it is a puzzle; I have seen the pieces so often that I may recognize them sooner than some people, but my main job is just to get them on the table. . . . Above all, I hope to leave you knowing that you never have to wait for all the pieces to be in place before you act.[3]

This is particularly troublesome for parents and kids who think that first and foremost they must be nice (don't make waves) instead of good (make the right kind of waves), that making a decision before you have all the information might mean hurting someone's feelings, and that's what we're supposed to avoid.

I know people who, without knowing all the "pieces" regarding Y2K, made substantial changes to their financial assets. In hindsight, they overreacted. But they did what they thought was best at the time with something very valuable to them, and they owe no apology for making an important choice without knowing every fact.

For some reason that escapes my understanding many parents think it's wrong for our children to behave this way or for us to behave this way on behalf of our children. What's more valuable to us than our kids?! The fact is, if we protected our children the way we protect our assets, most would be better off most of the time. Do we really love money more than our children? No one wants to reach that conclusion, yet why are we willing to ruffle feathers over money and not over our precious boys and girls?

Sound financial management means looking at the available facts and behaving accordingly. Let's look at the available facts of sexual abuse and do the same.

One in three girls and one in six boys will have sexual contact with an adult—usually a family member. About 20 percent of the time, the abuser is an adolescent. According to the National Institute of Mental Health, the average molester of girls will have about fifty victims before being caught and convicted. The average molester of boys will have 150 victims before being caught and convicted. Most will have "plenty after being caught as well, some even victimizing as many as 300 children during their 'careers.'"[4]

More than 90 percent of the offenders are heterosexual males who gained access to and control of the child. They count on secrecy and nice manners—that is, that your child will do as she is told and not fight back. Sexual predators do more than assault children physically. They hack into their minds and tell them lies are true ("If your mother knew, she'd hate you"). They deliberately try to erode a child's understanding of healthy boundaries and safety ("If you tell anyone, I'll kill you").

Many parents (myself included) have never experienced sexual abuse. That someone would behave so cruelly and diabolically is mind-boggling. But then I analyzed the malicious behavior I have experienced or witnessed in life, and you know what's remarkable? In every premeditated, malicious act, once the victim talked, the predator attacked the victim's comprehension of fairness, justice, and decency. Predators, sexual or otherwise do not, without force, admit to their cruelty and deception—they escalate their attack in order to maintain control.

> **"A CHILD MUST KNOW THAT HIS PARENTS WON'T BE DEVASTATED BY ANYTHING HE TELLS THEM."**
> —GAVIN DE BECKER

The greatest line of defense against sexual abusers continuing their behavior is for children to know they can bring their problems and concerns to parents and other adults who care for them, and that they are not met with criticism or additional punishment.

A child must know that his parents won't be devastated by anything he tells them. The knowledge that parents are strong enough to deal with whatever happens is a gift millions of today's adults didn't grow up with—such that many *still* haven't told their parents about abuse they suffered.[5]

Note the words "strong enough." In order to find the border-crossing between protection and overprotection, *we parents need all the strength we can find within ourselves, imparted from others, or given to us from God.* When we take action from a position of strength, our perspective is sound, and we are far less likely to underreact or overreact to provocation.

Also, consider signing up for the National Alert Registry to find out where registered sex offenders live in your area. Though this Web site is not foolproof (some sex offenders get away with not registering themselves), it can provide you with important information. Through *www.registeredoffenderslist.org/national-alert registry.htm* we discovered that one nearby neighborhood has a number of registered sex offenders. Our children don't play there.

## STRIKE EUPHEMISMS

Telling a little girl that no one should touch her in the areas a bikini covers is better than nothing but far from sufficient. Some sexual predators don't even want to touch kids—they want kids to touch them.

When we tell kids to beware of "sick people in the world," some think predators are those who cough all the time and have runny noses. When we tell them "bad people" hurt kids, they have no reason to be cautious with family members. What kid thinks a family member is "bad"?

Euphemisms make life more dangerous for kids. They kick sand over the line we're trying to find. *Be straightforward.* Tell your children that others should not:

- ▶ Put their hands down your pants or up your skirt
- ▶ Touch your private parts, even through clothes or pajamas
- ▶ Ask you to touch their private parts or ask you to remove their clothes
- ▶ Take off your clothes
- ▶ Take pictures of you with your clothes off
- ▶ Take off their clothes in front of you
- ▶ Show you pictures/movies of people doing sexual acts
- ▶ Talk about sexual behavior with you.

## BE THEIR DEFENDER

Child predators bank upon our nice, non-assertive responses so common among "good" Christians. And since many are people we know, including family members, we give them all the education they need about us. They test our boundaries to see whether or not we possess a protective power. Do you?

Being a Christian doesn't mean hovering above the ugliness of life. It means we are given the weapons necessary to face wickedness with the hope of creating something good in its place. Notice I didn't use the euphemism *tools,* a common word for this work. Law enforcement doesn't use *tools* to protect the peace. When weapons are required, parents shouldn't use *tools* either.

Violence is a fact of life. You aren't required to use violence in response to it. But if you want to be a truly good parent, you must use force and power when they're needed. Being forbearing in the face of perversion victimizes you and those in your care.

Knowing that most sexual predators are male, I foster in my head a healthy skepticism about every male who comes into our home. I even monitor family members. I look for lives that are out-of-balance, remarks that are out of place and inappropriate. Stares that linger too long, eyes that appear calculating when everyone else's aren't. I look for two-faced living, someone who is nice to me but rude to someone else. And I rarely trust someone without a sense of humor.

I subscribe to the belief that lions keep leopards tame. For good or for bad, I'm the guy with the power in my home. I'm the heavy sometimes. When used well, that's more powerful than actual weapons anyway. And actual weapons won't stop the kind of abuse we're combating. But keen perception and perseverance will.

## THE WILL TO RESPECT *AND* CHALLENGE AUTHORITY

We've seen that one of the best lines of true defense is teaching your child how to be assertive, since sex offenders prey on those who aren't. They look for kids who exhibit vulnerability through poor eye contact and shy body language, for kids who are too trusting with adults.

"Kids being assertive" means that sometimes your child should be allowed to defy the wishes of adults. I know this goes against most every fiber in the being of many traditional religious people who have been told to raise their children to submit to all authority (though Jesus did not—see how He behaved toward the Pharisees). But we're not talking legitimate authority. We're talking corrupt, malicious authority. We're talking misspent power and control. We're talking manipulation and deceit.

Let your child possess a will that dictates who she likes and who she doesn't. Do not constantly override this will. For example, if she recoils from a stranger for reasons unclear to you, do not make her apologize or go into the person's arms anyway. Instead, try to find out why she responded this way—it could be an early-warning system, and at any rate it's an opportunity for you to hear from her and understand her.

I've had dogs that refused to be friendly and warm to aggressive or nasty people. They keep a wary eye. If only we adults could be so perceptive.

Let me give an example. One of my children didn't want to go into the arms of a relative who was in a foul mood. His face was angry. His body was tense. He looked unwelcoming to me, and he must have looked terrifying to my child. "Looks like he doesn't want to go to you," I said.

My son defied the will of an adult, and I didn't correct him. I honored his healthy will, his boundaries, his desire to not go into the embrace of someone who repelled him. I honored his intuition about another person's presence and state of mind.

Always disciplining a child or overriding his will in order to please or appease adults (and, if we're honest, we do this sometimes to save face in public, not because we're concerned about our child's willfulness) is a sure way to make him *more* likely to be abused. Not all defiance is bad. Our children need to wield the sword of defiance against dark forces—few of which, by the way, are more powerful than adolescent peer pressure, which we'll soon examine. Sometimes defiance announces the beginning of moral courage, which we'll discuss at length later.

# THE DANGERS OF A "NICE" CHRISTIAN UPBRINGING

Sometimes it's best to let the spiritually wounded speak for themselves:

> I was bullied a lot in school and in church. I come from an extremely religious background. Our pastor was very controlling. My parents were leaders in the church, and we always had to be very careful with what people thought about us. My dad was the perfectionist type, with false humility. He always apologized when we had a conflict with others, saying, "I'm sorry my kids are so bad," even if it was the other person's fault. My mom was the daughter of an alcoholic and tried to fix problems she couldn't fix, and needed other people's approval too much. I remember as a child feeling responsible for her sadness and anger. I still feel responsible if someone is angry or upset with me, even if it's not my fault.
>
> I am the perfect Christian Nice Guy. My parents told me that God was very disappointed with me whenever I got angry about something. We weren't even allowed to

have disagreements in our home, so we learned how to be really sneaky. They told me that anger is a sin, even though I have looked for this idea in the Bible and I can't find it. I'm always smiling and gentle. Everyone says what a nice guy I am and how they could never imagine me being rude or angry. I am very polite, but it's driven by a deep sense of fear and shame. I try to be nice and perfect in order to avoid offending someone so I will not be scolded or rejected or have my weaknesses pointed out.

I am a coward. Many people would say this isn't true, but they don't know what happens inside me. I'm involved in many ministries, but I know the things I avoid. I am thirty, married, and have a stepdaughter. They are both very straightforward about what they think and feel, and they have helped me be more open and honest. But I still walk around with a lot of anxiety, dread, shame, self-doubt, and feelings of inferiority.

I know I shouldn't live in fear of man and should instead be concerned with doing God's will, but I fear making a mistake or being humiliated when I try to do the right thing.

Yeah, I'm a mess. Most people think I'm great, but they don't know the hell I go through.

This man's story, which includes a profoundly negative spiritual component, is common at Good Guy Ministries.[1] Most such adult struggles can be traced back with painful detail to spiritual education. If you want to raise confident, courageous, and successful children, you'll want to avoid the underreported spiritual pitfalls explained in this chapter.

The people to whom I provide individual instruction have noticeable talents and abilities. Many are more talented than they realize, more talented than they will allow themselves to admit. For example, one popular Christian speaker has a potent testimony about the power of forgiveness, but she's unable to spread her life-changing message to more people because of her spiritual education. She was told throughout childhood that believers should shun accomplishment in order to remain humble and avoid becoming prideful. Her success in ministry is causing her great internal turmoil, the main reason she hasn't been in public for some time now. Her well-meaning but naïve and destructive life-script has stopped her from sharing sparkling insights that set people free from hatred and bitterness.

*Yes,* these people have noticeable talents and abilities. But, of course, so do their peers. The fearful and the timid compete for jobs and spouses with one hand tied behind their back. They possess a self-handicap: They won't allow themselves to live successfully, in large part because they don't think God wants them to be successful.

These nice Christians who grew up as nice kids don't finish last—that's a common misconception that blurs the real problem. Nice Christians finish in life's frustrated middle, never getting to abundance, filled with inner angst, always playing defense, and usually filling out divorce papers at least once (sometimes more) during their beleaguered lifetime. Some never get to marriage because they're so nice as to be unattractive to potential spouses. Their passive approach toward life often leads them to the passive worlds of fantasy and pornography.

I've instructed attorneys, artists, doctors, landscapers, even a Sunday school teacher whose students would not respect him. Each is thoughtful, considerate, and warm. Many possess abilities that others crave. Yet each has a soul controlled by timidity, fear, and anxiety.

They usually hadn't much considered their backgrounds and experiences until their lives fell apart. They didn't seek or find help before they fell in love, married, had children, a mortgage, ailing parents. There were warning signs, but they didn't see them or, more commonly, refused to see them, until the amassed pressure they felt was so powerful they could nearly forge diamonds from it. In many ways, the foundation of their adulthood crash was laid, brick by well-meaning brick, by what they were told as children about God.

Take Lynne Hybels, who along with her husband, Bill, started Willow Creek Community Church in 1975, today one of the nation's most innovative ministries. In her book *Nice Girls Don't Change the World,* she describes a spiritual heritage that unintentionally makes children timid and passive, kids who do not make the world a better place. They are handicapped adults and ineffective Christians.

Hybels grew up in a small Michigan town and attended church regularly. She heard preaching that was "pretty much hellfire and brimstone. I heard a lot about sin and punishment, guilt and shame."[2]

Her training gave her "an uncanny ability to keep almost everybody happy almost all the time," though she didn't truly seem happy herself. As a little girl she was always smiling, though she doesn't remember ever hearing herself laugh. No one would have ever accused her of being "wildly in love with life," but she had "such a nice smile." She remembers being a very caring person, "though in a passive sort of way." She was "not the type to turn the world upside down."[3]

She always felt God was judging her and making her conform to a list of rules.

> At age ten I traded my ballet slippers for a flute because I had been taught that dancing was a sin but making music was an acceptable form of worship. . . . If there were rules to follow, I followed them. If there were pleasures to give up, I gave them up. If there was work to do, I did it. I was determined to earn God's love.[4]

She received the kind of education that derails adult life. She eventually grew despondent, exhausted, and depressed.

I was 39 years old when I walked into my counselor's office and said, "I've been working so hard to keep everybody else happy, but I'm so miserable I want to die." I spent the decade of my forties digging out of that hole. Now, nearly midway through my fifties, I've discovered that growing up is an ongoing process—I have not yet arrived. Still, I have learned some things on the journey to becoming a good woman.[5]

Part of this spiritual journey was figuring out what her gifts were—and what they weren't. She made halfhearted stabs to bring her life more in line with her gifts, but her training interfered with her ability to forge a more God-glorifying life. True to her nice Christian girl script, she didn't ask for help and, though she was surrounded by insightful and helpful Christians, she made sure not to inconvenience others with her frustrations or doubts, and she felt obligated to do whatever others asked her to do— regardless of whether or not she could do it well.

Lynne Hybels, a dyed-in-the-wool Christian Nice Girl, spent decades ignoring, neglecting, and denying her true gifts and passions, which drained her of the very vitality to which her husband was first drawn. She felt "incompetent and insecure. So my husband didn't win" either. Nor did her children. "They didn't get a joyful mother. They didn't get a fun mother. They didn't get to see, up close and personal, a woman fully alive in God."[6]

Like so many believing adults with a similar upbringing, she knew what she should do but lacked the backbone to do it.

God gave me a unique perspective and worthy dreams. God gave me words and influence to use for good. But I didn't use them. I didn't show up. I might have been there physically, but my gifts—my soul—didn't show up. I didn't value what I had to offer enough to actually offer it.[7]

She wasn't showing up and she didn't value her talents because she struggled mightily to overcome fear, as every person does when she receives her spiritual legacy. Fear lies to us, concealing the truth about who we are, the gifts we possess, and the goodwill of other people. Fear says we're too dumb or too amateurish or too wimpy to carry out the good works God puts before us. Fear, Hybels says, told her she "might as well give up."[8]

Listen to her hard-won insights into the difference between a *nice* Christian girl and a *good* Christian woman:

> Whereas a girl of any age lives out the script she learned as a child—a script too often grounded in powerlessness— a woman acknowledges and accepts her power to change, and grow, and be a force for good in the world.
>
> Whereas a nice girl tends to live according to the will of others, a good woman has only one goal: to discern and live out the will of God.
>
> A good woman knows that her ultimate calling in life is to be part of God's plan for redeeming all things in this sin-touched world.
>
> A good woman knows she cannot be all things to all people, and she may, in fact, displease those who think she should just be nice. She is not strident or petty or demand- ing, but she does live according to conviction. She knows that the Jesus she follows was a revolutionary who never tried to keep everyone happy.
>
> That picture of a good woman made me want to be one. It made me want to grow up and trade the innocuous acceptability of niceness for the world-changing power and passion of true goodness.[9]

Lynne Hybels went outside the advice many Christians receive at church, and it restored her life. After much grappling—which included realizing that for many years her children and husband had not gotten the kind of mother or wife she wished she was— she came out the other end of her training with a new approach toward life.

I'm happy for her, even though I also wish she didn't have to go through her ordeal. She emerged on the other side wiser and stronger. But others with her spiritual heritage aren't so fortunate. They struggle through a life that to them is serial disappointment and unending frustration. This is what can happen when someone receives that kind of "nice Christian upbringing." Here's what made them timid and weak instead of bold and courageous.

## WORM THEOLOGY

Many believers were given what's called worm theology. The name comes from the Isaac Watts hymn "Alas! And Did My Savior Bleed," one line of which says, "Would He

> **WORM THEOLOGY CONVOLUTES LOW SELF-WORTH WITH HUMILITY.**

devote that sacred head for such a worm as I?" Those who adhere to this view of life contend that low self-worth means God is more likely to show mercy and compassion upon them. *Worm theology convolutes low self-worth with humility.*

Many were told as kids that they are worthless in and of themselves—that they possess no inherent value, even though the Bible says that all people are created in God's image, endowing them with innate value and worth. Making matters worse is that people who come from tough childhood experiences such as abuse and neglect have what a counselor friend calls shame Velcro. They are actually attracted to systems of belief that demean them.

After speaking to an audience in Boston, Dr. James Dobson was questioned by an elderly missionary. She said that God wants her to think of herself as being no better than a "worm," and that, by way of implication, Dobson was wrong to say children should grow up with a quiet self-respect and confidence in themselves. Dobson and others who work to correct this false view of human worth are fighting a mighty battle. "That teaching," writes

Dobson of worm theology, "did not come from Scripture."[10]

Worm theology pulls a child down, filling her with nagging insecurities about her value and significance. It's as if parents, genuinely concerned that their children will grow up prideful and arrogant, want to make sure that this won't happen; however, instead of helping their kids build self-respect and confidence in humility, their instruction and discipline ensure that life will pass them by, leading to bitterness and sometimes rage toward the Lord.

The apostle Paul wrote that we shouldn't think more about ourselves than we ought; rather, we should use "sober judgment" in our self-assessment (Romans 12:3). Sober judgment means being realistic. It doesn't mean we should pretend we don't have gifts when we do, or that we should pretend we have talents, gifts, and abilities when we don't. Paul is telling us to be honest and realistic, not to despise ourselves.

Telling children they're worthless is the rhetoric of despair—especially during adolescence when worries of inferiority often hit their peak. And it's especially damaging to children who already think they're defective, that something is deeply wrong inside of them, not because they sin, but because *they* are "bad" and not as valuable as other kids. They won't allow themselves to believe they're good at anything; they will ward off compliments, and if people kick them around . . . well, isn't that what happens to worthless objects?

One of the most common ways a child deals with feelings of worthlessness, writes Dr. Dobson, "is to surrender, completely and totally."

> [This person withdraws into a] shell of silence and loneliness, choosing to take no chances or assume unnecessary emotional risks. This person would never initiate a conversation, speak in a group, enter a contest, ask for a date, run for election, or even defend his honor when it is tram-

pled. . . . As comedian Jackie Vernon once said, "The meek shall inherit the earth, because they'll be too timid to refuse it."[11]

Dale Ryan is CEO of Christian Recovery International, the parent organization of the National Association for Christian Recovery. Many of the people seeking help struggle with this understanding of God and are unable to live whole, God-glorifying lives. Ryan writes:

> Does God avoid us because we are sinners? If you have any doubt, any hesitation, about the answer to this question, I urge you to go back to the Bible. Did God avoid us? Is it not just the opposite? Did not God come to us? When God saw our pain, our brokenness, our defects of character, our insanity, what did God do? God came. Here. To be with us. To save us. To make a new kind of life possible for us. God's holiness is not the fragile kind that would be tainted by contact with broken, bent, damaged people. Blessed be the God and Father of our Lord Jesus Christ, who did not hide himself from our hopeless situation. God saw. God came—not to punish, not to nag, not to shame. Thank God that we were not worthless "worms" to God! We were, and are, precious, valuable. Wanted, a source of delight to God. That's just basic Bible. It may take a long time for this truth to sink in, but it's not really fancy theology. It's Christianity 101. . . .
>
> We have learned very broken ways to think and feel about ourselves. In recovery we struggle not to just think better about ourselves, but to do an honest self-assessment. . . . Part of this self-assessment involves doing a "fearless moral inventory." The content of our inventory can be a pretty discouraging and disturbing list. But the process of doing our inventory is to be characterized by fearlessness. What does "fearless" mean? Certainly it means that we will be courageous while working on our inventory. But more specifically it means that we will seek

to be so secure in God's love for us that no matter what we find in our inventory, we will know that we are still loved, still valuable, still of infinite importance to our Higher Power. It is only love that can sustain us when we experience the fear that comes from shame, from rejection, from resentments and from guilt. We seek to do a fearless inventory because we want God to so fill us with love that little room remains for fear. May God grant you the grace this day to think and feel about yourself in ways that are consistent with how your loving and grace-full Father thinks and feels about you.[12]

# WHAT KIND OF PRIDE IS WRONG?

Jim, a talented artist, did not take a promotion at work that would have allowed his wife to stay home with their children, a dream of hers, because he didn't think he was good enough for the job, even when multiple supervisors assured him he was. "I was told as a kid in my Christian home that I shouldn't go around thinking I was better than other kids. But I was better at art than other kids. My teachers told me. But I pretended I wasn't."

Jim denied his gift instead of embracing it. Like so many Christian Nice Guys, Jim lives with one foot on the gas, the other on the brakes. He wastes tremendous amounts of energy trying to resolve inner dialogues that haunt him. He wants to be the best artist he can be, yet he thinks God doesn't want him to be successful. He has the tools necessary to provide well for his family, but he's waiting for God's permission to thrive. He's waiting for the green light, but his spiritual training says it's going to stay red.

Such strugglers were told that believing you're good at something makes you "worldly." I remember one preacher's family that lived out this principle. When their son once told his ten-year-old sister, "I'm good at baseball," she scolded, "You're not supposed to say that—it's bragging."

Being a coach, that was especially sad for me to witness. As kids grow up and play at higher levels, they become pretty well physically matched and similarly skilled. What often makes the difference in an athlete is his belief in himself, which helps him approach his sport with confidence. This *can* spill into arrogance (as anyone who watches professional sports has seen), and arrogance isn't good. But false humility isn't good, either. Like arrogance, self-denigration is dishonesty about who we are, and it easily spills over into unfulfilled potential, leading to anguish and, if unchecked, bitterness.

This concern isn't limited to athletics. For instance, I am continually grateful that Clive Staples Lewis did not grow up in the kind of "nice" Christian home that teaches children to pretend their gifts are merely average. The world may well have been deprived of the blessings wrought through his phenomenal talents had fake humility and false piety been foisted upon him; these fallacies sink so many believers from being agents of true redemption. C. S. Lewis *did* notice these distortions within Christian circles, and he opposed them:

> We may be content to remain what we call "ordinary people": but He is determined to carry out a quite different plan. To shrink back from that plan is not humility: it is laziness and cowardice. To submit to it is not conceit or megalomania; it is obedience.[13]

More than a hundred biblical passages warn against pride, the sin of self-sufficiency. Yet we must take care to understand what we're actually being warned against: haughtiness, contempt, arrogance, self-aggrandizement, the idea that we need nothing and no one. This is *false* belief about ourselves—belief that we're something we're not. And that's pride.

Conversely, *believing, affirming, and embracing who we truly are, who God made us to be, and how He has gifted us, is not pride.* That is honesty, that is wisdom, and, as Lewis said, that is obedience.

Haughtiness, contempt, and arrogance stop us from loving God, our neighbor, and ourselves. Says Dobson:

A haughty person is too pompous to bow humbly before the Creator, confessing sins and submitting to a life of service to Him. Such arrogance produces hatefulness toward others, disregarding their feelings and needs.[14]

Dobson does not believe that

the Bible condemns an attitude of quiet self-respect and dignity. Certainly those responses could not represent the pinnacle of the seven deadliest sins. Jesus commanded us to love our neighbors as ourselves, implying that we are permitted a reasonable expression of self-love. In fact, true love for others is impossible until we experience a measure of self-respect. . . . Some people actually believe that Christians should maintain an attitude of self-hatred in order to avoid the pitfall of haughtiness.[15]

# DON'T DEFEND YOURSELF?

Many Christians were told as children that all forms of conflict are wrong. Their religious instruction included the command never to respond when others tried to hurt them emotionally with words, physically with fists, or relationally with lies and rumors. They were to accept abuse because it was from God's hand to form character in them (most notably, humility). When they were bullied at school, they were told they were being persecuted for righteousness' sake, even when the abuse had nothing to do with morality.

Complicating matters is that many came from homes that either avoided conflict completely. (Or, they witnessed violent and abusive conflict; either way, they never saw conflict handled constructively.) In their environments, conflict was swept under the rug, and they were schooled in the ways of peace-faking, not peacemaking. They didn't witness how well-handled conflict can bless an individual or an entire family, and they didn't learn that conflict will be a part of every life lived well. As a result, these children as adults often have disastrous marriages, entered into with naïve beliefs and stunted relational abilities.

In stark contrast to this way of life, both the Old and New Testaments are replete with conflict, often accompanied with God's approval and favor. However, Paul's admonishment "If it is possible, as far as it depends on you, live at peace with everyone" (Romans 12:18) has been taken to mean that we should never "disturb the peace."

**PARENTS WHO TEACH THEIR CHILDREN THAT ALL CONFLICT IS WRONG ARE TELLING THEIR KIDS THAT BEING A PUNCHING BAG WILL SOMEHOW SHOW OTHERS CHRISTIAN LOVE.**

Here's something we need to know: this is absolutely true, *when it applies to actual peace*. Where there is real peace, we are to *keep* peace. But where there is not peace, we are to *make* peace, and that can require conflict. Peace is not merely the absence of tumult; peace means that things have been made right, and where they have not been made right, it is *wrong* to pretend perpetually that there is peace, justice, respect, and goodwill (see, for example, Jeremiah 6:14).

Parents who teach their children that all conflict is wrong are telling their kids that being a punching bag will somehow show others Christian love. True peace, true justice, true respect, and true goodwill become distorted for these kids, and they often become doormats. Even when they reach adulthood, a deceitful boss is likely to sniff them out, employ them, and mistreat them, knowing they won't speak up or push back. He knows they won't point out real problems or walk into conflict, because they mistake retaliation for self-defense.

"Turning the other cheek" does *not* mean we aren't allowed to defend ourselves. It means, for example, that we are not to return an insult with an insult—it means we aren't to respond to evil with evil. When I share this with Christian Nice Guys, a palpable sigh usually fills our conversation. Then a common anger, mingled with shame, comes out of men when they think about what they allowed others to do to them without resistance.

As a parent, you've probably experienced that doing the right thing in life doesn't always earn applause. It can cause others to attack you even more. It takes tremendous backbone to stand up to such pressure. The only way you can pass that strength on to your children as you spiritually educate them is by continuing to cultivate it yourself.

When people follow Christ, they become neither pacifists nor Jihadists. We become truth bearers, redemption seekers—bearers of light in a world at war with the Real. We are called to exert our will, in line with God's, to carry out His purpose on earth. *Sometimes this includes conflict.* Our participation in God's redemptive work requires the tougher virtues, such as discipline, perseverance, and fortitude. We are required to use force justly, wisely, and in the service of love, which isn't always comfortable, pleasant, or nice.

## JUST GIVE IT TO JESUS?

Another hallmark of timid, ineffective living is the teaching that what a person needs to do is "give her problems to Jesus" and then get out of the way. This false premise negates the involvement of her will and her choices in forging spiritual maturity and moral fiber. One man who contacted me for help told me this when I started asking questions that pushed him out of his Nice-

Guy comfort zone: "Thank you. But all I really need to do is to give my problems to Jesus and let him do the work." This standard operating procedure of fearful people takes true facts about our faith—in this case Jesus' desire and ability to help us with our troubles—and manipulates them in order to hide from both terror of conflict and responsibility for actions.

God works *with* us to help us heal and mature and become more like His Son (e.g., see Romans 8:29; 2 Corinthians 3:18; Ephesians 2:10). His role is indispensable. But so is ours. Augustine described this in saying that man's will is to God's grace and direction "as the horse is to the rider." It takes both to get anywhere. God expects us to take an active role in our lives (e.g., see Matthew 7:5; 1 Corinthians 10:28; Philippians 2:12–13), through both intent and decisions.

Why are many kids told that their only "spiritual work" is praying and reading their Bibles, and that all else pretty much meddles with what God wants to do in them? Successful people who live abundantly don't think this way. They understand that their will and their choices have a large impact on the quality of their lives and on their ability to love and bless others. Writes Dallas Willard, professor of philosophy at USC:

> The enemy of our time is not human capacity, or over-activism, but the enemy is passivity—the idea that God has done everything and you are essentially left to be a consumer of the grace of God and that the only thing you have to do is find out how to do that and do it regularly. I think this is a terrible mistake and accounts for the withdrawal of active Christians from so many areas of life where they should be present. It also accounts for the lack of spiritual growth, for you can be sure that if you do not act in an advised fashion consistently and resolutely you will not grow spiritually. We all know that Jesus said, in John 15, "without me you can do nothing." We need to

add, "if you do nothing, it will be most assuredly without him."[16]

# BE WORD-WISE *AND* STREETWISE

As we've noted, much of today's Christianity overemphasizes gentle virtues and underemphasizes rugged virtues. The latter are essential in helping children mature in their faith and live abundant lives. Ignoring the broader council of God is spiritual neglect.

One example I give in workshops, seminars, and conferences is among the most potent and haunting statements Jesus made. He said, in sending His followers out into the world like sheep among wolves: "Be wise as serpents and innocent as doves" (Matthew 10:16 NRSV). The Greek word for "wise," *phronimos,* can likewise be translated as "cunning" or "shrewd." Jesus wants followers who are streetwise, who

> are on constant alert, looking for angles, surviving by their wits. I want you to be smart in the same way—but for what is *right*—using every adversity to stimulate you to creative survival, to concentrate your attention on the bare essentials, so you'll live, really live, and not complacently just get by on good behavior. (Luke 16:9 THE MESSAGE)

Almost sounds blasphemous, doesn't it? Not getting by on good behavior (complacency)? Not waiting for God's green light or miraculous intervention (passivity)? Not making sure we have all the right answers before making a decision (timidity)? Aren't these what being a Christian is all about? According to Jesus, in His own words, *no.*

Our need for this kind of wisdom—for both followers and leaders—is greater than we realize. Of the thirteen character traits the Barna Group tested for among more than 1,300 Christian leaders, wisdom came in dead last. We are perilously out of balance. Believers, beginning in Sunday school, wrongly have been told that piety alone will pave the road to an abundant, God-glorifying life. Jesus never said this. He wants us to marry virtuous living to wise living.

The problem for many of us is that wise living isn't always comfortable or pleasant. A wise person is sometimes hard to get along with. And a wise parent sometimes appears mean. Says Marilyn Chandler McEntyre:

> One of my husband's finer moments in parenting came one day when, after he had uttered an unwelcome word of correction to a disgruntled child, he leaned down, looked her in the eye, and said, "Honey, this is what love looks like." Love, in that case, must have seemed to her a far cry from nice.[17]

Here's another example. We often preach the virtue of generosity to our children without teaching an end to wise generosity. More so, a time when generosity with valuable things (God's holy Word, our resources, energy, and talents) is sinful: "Do not give what is holy to the dogs; nor cast your pearls before swine, lest they trample them under their feet, and turn and tear you in pieces" (Matthew 7:6 NKJV). How can one tell the difference between smart generosity and stupid generosity? You guessed it: the wisdom of serpents, which we aren't born with. We need to learn more about it so we can practice it—starting in Sunday school.

Why is valuable wisdom so rare? I don't know all the answers, but I know a few. Wisdom, like humility, helps us see life more clearly. With this clarity comes inevitable decisions: for instance, continue down a sinful path, or repent by turning from lies and move in a God-glorifying direction. The choice seems easy until you count the cost. For many, wisdom is too demanding—it often requires change. We often prefer our illusions.

Virtuous living without wise living is not only wasteful, it may well make you an accomplice to evil, as drug counselors demonstrate when well-meaning family members enable kin to continue their destructive lifestyles. Personal piety may give the impression that we're doing good works when we really aren't. Marry virtue to wisdom during the spiritual training of your children; then you'll truly be giving them the tools they need for a successful life and increase their ability to bless others as well.

Parents, during your own Bible study, keep track of the wisdom you obtain. Then take the easiest example to understand and share it with your children. (I do this at dinnertime.) This will lead to great conversations and spiritual enlightenment.

If you doubt the accuracy of my claim, do a little exam. How many sermons have you heard on how to be shrewd and street-smart (wise as a serpent)? Chances are, not many (or none). How many have you heard on devotion and being pleasant and agreeable (innocent as a dove)? Jesus never said one aspect was more important than the other, but today's church usually does.

It can also be illuminating to keep track of and compare how many times you're encouraged to emulate the gentle virtues (gentleness, meekness, humility, and so on) and how many times you're encouraged to emulate the rugged virtues (boldness, courage, bravery, and so on). I've been doing this for some time and the results are shocking. Again, *we are ignoring the broader council of God, and lives are being destroyed because of it.*

## SHOWING OUR KIDS THE WHOLE SPECTRUM OF VIRTUE

As mentioned before, wisdom often leads to conflict, and it is spiritually neglectful not to explain to our children that if they align their lives with God's will, they will be met with challenges.

If we don't, we can be sure we'll be raising a generation of what I call Second-Seed people—those who walk away from their faith when the going gets tough.

When we read Jesus' parable of the sower (Matthew 13; Mark 4; Luke 8), which describes why faith grows in some but not others, we hope we'll only find our inner lives described in one key passage. When we find our faithlessness laid bare on the page, we sometimes fail to understand the real reason: We simply don't have the backbone to withstand the difficulties that come from being the oddballs God wants us to be.

Second-Seed people respond superficially to God's Word.

> These are the ones sown on rocky ground: when they hear the word, they immediately receive it with joy. But they have no root, and endure only for a while; then, when trouble or persecution arises on account of the word, immediately they fall away. (Mark 4:16–17 NRSV).

They lack the rugged virtue of fortitude. Why? Because their training makes them so eager to please others that they crumple under even mild criticism. They were trained to be nice kids instead of good ones.

Such people may possess a saving knowledge of Jesus, but they do not follow Him closely. This is what's caused by an anxious mindset born from spiritual neglect: It depletes people of their rootedness and brings fearfulness, though "God did not give us a spirit of timidity, but a spirit of power, of love and of self-discipline" (2 Timothy 1:7). Passive, worried people are being shaped by someone other than God; they are being made into the image of their life experiences, starting in childhood. We parents need to stop creating spiritual veal and give our kids the training they need—the harder but more rewarding endeavor of creating true spiritual warriors.

I see this, generally, in our teaching children about love. When we encourage them to be more loving, we usually encourage them to do nice things for others. We must also show them that love includes caring so much about someone that you confront him when he's wrong and defend him when he's under attack.

Fortunately, a growing cluster of writers are reconsidering our current portrayal of Jesus and Christian faith as a conflict-free existence; they are, as Mark Galli claims, "filling in the picture." Galli, managing editor of *Christianity Today,* is among the bright lights emancipating Jesus from well-meaning yet hazardous sermons, books, and songs that portray Him as history's all-time Nicest Guy.

In *Jesus Mean and Wild: The Unexpected Love of an Untamable God,* Galli is quick to point out that he does not live up to the rugged ideals he finds in the life of Christ and in the admonishments of virtuous Christian behavior.

> My family and friends tell me that I do indeed live out Jesus' "mean and wild" love—courage, boldness, righteous anger, etc.—more than many people. But I still feel that I am addicted to niceness, and that there are many instances when my courage to act in love fails me. So I'm looking to Jesus to help me grow in this area.[18]

Galli wrote this powerful book to address a subculture in many churches that emphasizes the gentler . . . virtues, which are great, but sometimes don't address the tougher virtues like courage and boldness. This subculture puts out sermons where we hear how Jesus never got angry, never lost His cool, never said a mean thing and was always patient. This isn't what you find in the Gospels. I personally was stunned by His boldness and anger found in the Gospels, especially the Gospel of Mark.[19]

This subculture that creates troubled adults needs to see another side of love, which takes a variety of forms.

You learn this pretty quickly as a parent. A good parent is tender and tough, depending on what his child needs. We have a hard time translating this truth into our adult lives when we relate to God. Sometimes God is stiff and tough with us because He loves us. He's not being abusive. Athletes tend to understand this concept better than the rest of the population.[20]

Galli says we ignore tougher biblical passages because they make us uncomfortable.

A lot of this discomfort revolved around the misconceptions by some Christians that anger and conflict are always wrong and that Jesus is always nice. We need to topple this false idol of Jesus that we've made. [The real Jesus is the same one who] invites those who are weary and heavy-laden to come to Him for rest. What we all have to learn is that Jesus' love comes to us in a variety of ways; sometimes it feels good; sometimes it doesn't. But if we give it time, we'll see that many of the things that didn't feel good were really God's means of shaping us, preparing us, disciplining us, loving us.[21]

A merely Sweet Savior is ultimately incapable of helping us— and our children—in life's most difficult moments.

I need a Savior who empathizes with my pain, but I also need a Savior who is strong to save—who has the power to defeat satanic influences in my life, who will overcome evil in the world one day. In the end, the Sweet Savior merely feels bad for me but is helpless in the face of evil. If we only show children, especially boys, His compassion, they may be tempted to think of Jesus as a wimp—certainly not someone worth giving their lives to. And if we show only the "mean and wild" side, they may become merely arrogant and abusive.[22]

In addition, showing children only the Nice Nazarene runs

the risk of making them sentimental instead of truly compassionate.

They give evil a pass instead of confronting it boldly. They become nice instead of loving. To leave this dimension of a tough Jesus out of our spiritual education is to misrepresent Jesus, and that can only create crippled disciples.[23]

Weak and timid children become adults whose lives are often riddled with relational havoc, whose spouses do not respect them. This letter from a reader of my previous book, *Married . . . But Not Engaged,* shows how deadly lack of self-respect and respect are to marriages and how true marital harmony is created when a more assertive approach toward life is employed.

*I just wanted to share with you the journey that my husband and I have embarked upon thanks to your book.*

*He failed to come through on his word to me about something, not something big, but still I was angry and felt let down. In previous times, his apologies to me have mostly consisted of his begging for my forgiveness. Although I love him with all my heart, I have, at those times, held onto my anger out of fear of being let down again and have not forgiven him straightaway as I should have done.*

*Last night, though, was so different. With his characteristic sincerity, he apologized, took full responsibility for the fact that he had let me down, but he did not beg! For the first time in our marriage of almost five years, I was able to admit to him that I felt I couldn't express my anger to him for fear that he couldn't handle it. I was able to honestly express my feelings of anger.*

*At the same time, I understood from the calm, self-respecting way he was speaking that my usual withholding of forgiveness would be entirely useless. He had apologized and was willing to make restitution, but he would not be manipulated—and his life was not "over" until I was happy with him again.*

*I felt like I'd been pulled up short. I looked at my past behavior and didn't like what I saw. I recognized that while he would crawl and beg and grovel, I felt justified in my disrespectful treatment of him. After all, he obviously didn't feel he deserved respect! But last night, when he treated himself with respect, I couldn't help but give him that same dignity. I felt a new respect for him welling up in me and I let go of my anger.*

*Now we're both excited. I'm reading your book along with him so that I can encourage and support his growth, and mine!*

*We have a baby boy and I feel like this is the perfect time for this change to be happening. I'm so glad that my son will grow up with an example of what a man should be, and (hopefully) the treatment he deserves from his future wife. We are both grateful for your much-needed message!*

Weak and timid children become parents whose children find them spineless and unreliable. They have checkered employment histories and an obligatory church attendance that fuels cynicism and resentment toward God. These anxious people also wear their bodies out—they're more at risk for hypertension, migraines, intestinal maladies, and other stress-related illnesses.

Perhaps the most shocking part of their personality, already entrenching itself while they're kids, is that they tend to be dishonest and deceptive. Because their parents cannot or will not discern the difference between false humility born of timidity and real humility created by genuine modesty, they don't point out to their children what fear and passivity are doing to their lives. So for example, when they lose at a board game or at pickup hoops because their timidity prohibits them from cultivating playfulness and competitiveness, they say they lost because "I didn't try my hardest," and "I could have won if I wanted to." These are the words I heard a pastor's passive son tell my boy. They develop ways to deceive themselves and others in ways that can set patterns and strongholds for their entire lives.

Furthermore, they frequently feel they have no choice in the matter, because their only option is to conform to the will and expectations of others. They've been robbed of their ability to do what they believe is right. For instance, when they witness other children being bullied, they watch as if it's occurring on TV or as if they're not even present. They lack the tougher virtues, and it's the tougher virtues they *must* have.

# TRUTH ABOUT BULLIES
# AND VICTIMS

*On December 1, 1997, fourteen-year-old Michael Carneal, a*
*bespectacled ninth-grader, walked into Heath High School in West*
*Paducah, Kentucky, carrying a large parcel wrapped in a quilt. He*
*lied and told a somewhat suspicious teacher that the bundle contained*
*"props for a science project." Shortly before 8:00 A.M., just before*
*the first bell rang, this son of a respected lawyer and elder put down*
*his bundle, inserted earplugs, drew a weapon, and fired twelve shots*
*into a circle of kids gathered for prayer in the lobby.*

*Students screamed and wept. Two girls lay dead. A third died a*
*short time later. Five others were hospitalized; two were partially*
*paralyzed.*

*"I'm sorry," Carneal calmly told principal Bill Bond, as another*
*student forced him to drop his gun and pinned him against a lobby*
*wall.*

*According to Bond, Carneal's school essays and short stories*
*revealed a recurring theme: He felt picked on, weak, and powerless.*

*The boy apparently "had been teased all his life" and "just struck out in anger at the world."*[1]

## CHILDREN WHO HAVE BECOME FEARFUL AND TIMID ARE PRIME TARGETS FOR BULLIES.

As we've seen, children who have become fearful and timid are prime targets for bullies. They haven't been trained in the ways of true courage and honest humility, and in their perceived powerlessness they are ill-equipped to handle the rough-and-tumble side of adolescent life (and, later, adult life). We parents need to better understand why certain kids are so often singled out, and we must learn what we can do to help these children escape the treachery of serial mistreatment.

We also need to tackle misconceptions like the belief that what doesn't kill us makes us stronger. Nihilism and Social Darwinism have fed us this line, which brings comfort to those who temporarily teeter on top of corrupt pecking orders but doesn't sit right with most anyone else. A voice within us, the voice of truth, tells us something much different. Like the parents who rush to their children's school the day of a violent catastrophe, we know that what's happening isn't the way things are supposed to be.

On October 11, 2006, a Japanese boy, still in junior high, wrote in his suicide note, "Bullying is to blame. I'm really serious. Goodbye." The only thing that had been "made stronger" in him was the conviction that he was worthless and weak. Rather than "what doesn't kill us makes us stronger," it might be better said that what is stronger can kill a soul's desire to live.

There *are* adults who believe that bullying makes kids stronger. But they're fooling themselves, perhaps literally so, in justifying their own cowardice and apathy. Here are the facts: Those who undergo intense and prolonged adolescent bullying often do not grow stronger. They become infused with anxiety and depression, with humiliation and soul-crushing self-reproach. They are turned into the metallic arms of isolation, where they can be buried under paranoia and despair. Some are buffeted with thoughts of revenge; some, in the furious rage of powerlessness, become homicidal and/or suicidal.

On September 29, 1998, in Arizona, Jared High committed suicide. He'd been mired in a major depressive episode brought on by his approximately eight-minute-long violent beating at the hands of a known bully in a school gymnasium. One doctor reported that High may have been within one hit of having his neck broken. He was just thirteen years old.

According to authors Neil Marr and Tim Field, approximately sixteen children commit suicide in England each year due to bullying, like sixteen-year-old James Rogers, who would come home from school with bruises and torn clothing and would eventually poison himself. The authors thrust a new word into our lexicon, "bullycide," which we will undoubtedly hear more about in the years to come.[2]

In order to help our children become confident, courageous, and successful, we must confront this hideous form of treatment that if unleashed upon an adult would put the perpetrator behind bars. As it stands today, due in part to its prevalence, bullies, these purveyors of torment, are sometimes unlikely even to get detention. Some signs of improvement do bring hope. For example, the state of South Carolina passed legislation, effective January 2007, that expands anti-bullying policies beyond the traditional ban on inflicting physical harm. New district policies now include bans on intimidation and other forms of emotional bullying, including cyber-harassment via cell phones and computers. I see here a fulfillment of the prophet Isaiah's command: "Learn to do right! Seek justice, encourage the oppressed" (Isaiah 1:17).

Sadly, though, this is still the exception. The injustice many kids experience on a regular basis is so extreme yet so accepted that in many ways it could qualify as the next stage of the civil rights movement. As with other unacceptable atrocities, my hope is that we as a culture will look back upon what we used to tolerate in this arena and say to ourselves, "What were we thinking?"

I wrote earlier that children need to feel bad sometimes in order to become confident and virtuous adults. By "bad," though, I mean moderate challenges, effectively doled out, that serve them with opportunities to analyze a problem, create a plan, execute a solution, and experience success. I *don't* mean that children need to feel miserable and despairing. There's a difference between a temporary setback and prolonged anguish. Between sadness and sadism. Between good-natured teasing and torrential torment. Many sufferers of bullying aren't challenged by their ordeal— they're squashed by it. And sometimes the bullied become the bullies, squashing others in their desperate attempts to feel empowered.

# BULLYING CREATES BROKENNESS . . . AND MORE BULLIES

The sins associated with bullying on school campuses do not only include the effects upon the victims who live in a constant state of fear and do not receive the education afforded to them by law. On that premise we can expect more lawsuits against school districts that fail to handle bullying effectively. Additionally, bullies who aren't confronted by peers and leaders don't receive the confrontation and correction they need to do well in life, and they often go on to bully as adults. They're prone toward spousal abuse, and 60 percent of boys named as bullies in grades six through nine have at least one court conviction by age twenty-four. Their chances of drug and alcohol abuse also increase dramatically.

Bullying is a timidity factory, because it fills bystanders, both peers and authority figures, who rarely intervene, with cowardice. Bullies provide others the opportunity to exercise courage and bravery, to grow their moral backbone. But these usually fail the test.

Cowardice is the enemy of courage. Cowardice makes us feel sludge-like; it erodes our integrity and our dignity; it mortifies our souls and diminishes our self-regard. Odd that we wouldn't already be focusing on this, in an age where self-esteem is an untouchable sacred cow. It seems we're all for bolstering self-esteem in our kids—until it comes to the exercise of courage, the virtue upon which all other virtues depend.

The U.S. military defines cowardice as "misbehavior before the enemy." It includes running away before an enemy and willfully failing to do all within one's power to fight or defend when it's his duty to do so. Cowardice's maximum punishment is the death penalty.

It's important not to take this next analogy too far, but we know that about 85 percent of school shootings have as their motive (1) revenge against bullies and (2) retaliation against authority that was perceived as failing to protect. It's not *always* unrestrained bullying—in many cases, authority did intervene and tried to curtail bullying. Yet teachers and school administrators as a whole are not as good at recognizing or combating bullying as they say, or as school districts want us to believe. Studies show that school officials are in a very real way "misbehaving before the enemy," and with increasing frequency a death penalty is being paid by others.

At the same time, like the levies in New Orleans, the line of defense comprised only of teachers and administrators is not strong enough to hold back the magnitude of this hurricane. Do teachers need more training and legal support to defend them when they do behave courageously? You bet. But why focus only on teachers and related staff? Why not peers, the majority of whom witness these acts and, by and large, do nothing helpful? As you'll see in chapter 9, they become part of the problem.

A good portion of the blame that goes toward teachers and administrations is a convenient rationalization for society's lack of courage and related virtue. The problem is far too large to blame on one group alone or on one line of defense. The levies are not built to withstand the pressure. They must be fortified with other material. We're that material.

# BULLYING DEFINED

The American Psychological Association estimates that a shocking 90 percent of fourth through eighth graders report being victims of some form of bullying. Sometimes parents (usually fathers), when they discover their kid is being kicked around, tell him to respond in kind. This is generally not good advice, though, because being bullied, by definition, means one person has more power than another, whether physical, verbal, social, financial, or whatever gives one power over another in a given culture. This is why the majority of school shooters shoot: they use technology in a desperate attempt to bridge and surmount the power gap.

Bullying, in most cases, is not when two kids of roughly equal power go toe to toe. Such a standoff, or face off, or square off, does not get a parent's disdain for injustice roaring. The state of inequality that's innate to bullying is why kids who are physically, verbally, or socially bullied must be shown more effective ways of handling their situation. Otherwise they will likely receive increasing humiliation, or worse.

Bullying deploys aggressive behavior with negative intent from a more powerful child to a lesser. This is why in many ways bullies are cowards: They launch their attacks of humiliation from a superior position with assurance of victory. The uneven playing field, tipped in their favor, emboldens them; bullies rarely go after someone of their own size in physical stature, verbal acumen, or social status. This is why adults must step in and level the field: fear and humiliation are as substantial obstacles to learning as poor nutrition, bad study habits, and lack of sleep. *Bullying often does not sort itself out naturally.*

Most bullying is not physical, but in other ways it still shoves, pushes, and punches. It's often social, like spreading rumors and lies about another through spoken or written words (via electronic media, called cyber-bullying). As a journalist, I'm amazed by what bullies think they can publish without considering their victim's rights under the law. Hubris is a blinding force that can be key to their defeat; as bullying among youth the world over receives more scrutiny, we can expect libel laws to modify and become more applicable.

A bully's teasing is not good-natured—it intends to sting, pierce, and degrade. Bullying is the use of power to marginalize, discredit, and exclude. It's not the putting up of boundaries against something dangerous or cruel; it's rejecting and abusing someone because she's different and frequently not as fortunate. Bullying is superior power wielded by an individual or group for unjust reasons and in unjust ways.

Churches are far from exempt, according to counselors who work with those bullied within congregations. Counselor and bullying expert Barbara Coloroso, after helping numerous people damaged from this form of mistreatment, says everyone who witnesses examples of bullying in churches, especially among leadership, has "an obligation to speak, to make the church a safe place."[3] She recommends that congregations develop a code of conduct and make it public. Otherwise, says the former Franciscan nun, "religion can be an instrument of" bullying, which has three common elements: the liberty to exclude, intolerance for difference, and a sense of entitlement.[4]

# BULLIES EXPOSED

Bullies are the most disliked group of children in any given classroom. The kids they pick on come in second (more on this later).

Bullies are often both abuser and abused. They frequently receive parenting that uses unhealthy force to get them to behave a certain way. School bullies are often bullied at home, where their will, wants, and desires are overridden and trampled. In turn, they override and trample others.

**SCHOOL BULLIES ARE OFTEN BULLIED AT HOME, WHERE THEIR WILL, WANTS, AND DESIRES ARE OVERRIDDEN AND TRAMPLED.** This is what Brigham Young University professors Clyde Robinson, David Nelson, and Craig Hart wanted people to understand from the results of the study that inspired the movie "Mean Girls." They concluded that much of children's behavior does not depend on their own thoughts but on the way they see their parents and older siblings acting at home.[5]

That helps explain the bewilderment, dismay, and anger some parents experience when they try to reason with a bully's parents. An appeal to a common good—respect for personal boundaries—isn't sufficiently respected by coercive parents. They don't believe or acknowledge that trampling occurs. To them, coercion is normal and natural, possibly even right. And their children are following suit.

A regular perception is that bullies have more testosterone in their bodies than others. One study shows the opposite: they actually possess less than bystanders and victims.[6] Hormones aren't required for the doling out of abuse. A deflated sense of others and an inflated view of self is far more common. Research shows that bullies possess a positive view of themselves even when their peers unanimously don't. More so, they actually believe their peers think highly of them as well. Their self-deception would likely be met with pity by other parents if it weren't for the behavior they unleash. Bullies in many ways are a tragic study in self-delusion.

## HELP FOR PARENTS OF BULLIES

► Bullies tend to come from parents who bully. Examine your parenting style to see if it contains coercion. If it does, begin to make things right.

► Help your child develop empathy by helping him learn to feel what others feel.

► Explain to her how her strengths should be used to help others, not hurt them.

► Look for warning signs. Bullies are always getting into scrapes, pretending they didn't play a role, and blaming their fights on others. "He started it" is a common lie.

► Help him express himself through language instead of physical intimidation.

► Ask him about his day, and then really listen. Smile.

► Give her physical affection.

Though bullying peaks in the middle-school years, it often doesn't end there. A Rowan University Study found that elementary school bullies frequently persist throughout their high school and college years.[7] Not surprisingly, physical bullying is replaced with verbal bullying, since physically assaulting another adult is far more likely to result in real trouble with the law.

Other characteristics of bullies:

▶ They do not take rejection to heart or learn from it the way other kids do.

▶ They deny their maladjustment and often blame others for their problems.

▶ Boys are more prone to physically bully; girls tend to bully by attacking social status and ties—through damaging, manipulating, or controlling their relationships.

▶ Female bullies are more likely to become mothers prone toward maternal irritability, says psychiatrist Sue Bailey. They're more likely to become teenage mothers, enter into violent relationships, and suffer infection and injuries.[8]

▶ A child who is a bully by age nine or ten—and possibly long before—is likely to remain a bully into adulthood.

▶ They have a strong desire to dominate.

▶ They lack empathy, the ability to fully grasp the feelings of others, and therefore come to deny the suffering of others.

▶ They are untroubled by anxiety, which can be a source of restraint when experienced in the right quantity.

▶ Up to sixth grade, they are of average popularity, which then sharply declines with each passing year. They tend to have two or three friends, usually other aggressive kids.

▶ By high school they are marginalized and not well-liked, which they don't usually realize.

▶ They're expert for their age in getting short-term payoffs, but lousy at long-term thinking and planning.

▶ Their verbal intelligence is lower than their peers.

▶ As they age they become increasingly selective with their targets.

► They're less interested in the speed of surrender than in the pomp of pain and suffering.

We currently call what bullies do "antisocial." This is true, but it's highly euphemistic. If adults experienced what school victims endure, they wouldn't call it antisocial—they'd label it *criminal*. Those who've been bullied in the workplace know how it drains their soul. For some absurd reason we collectively don't think such draining takes place with children, or if it does, that it's not as damaging.

# CYBER-BULLIES

Today, thanks to the blessing and curse of highly personalized electronic media, there's even less easy escape from bullying. Where students used to worry about being bullied at school, now beginning in middle school, they also fear that everyone at school will see them bullied all over cyberspace—for example, on My-Space or Xanga, or through instant messaging, text messaging, e-mail, blogs, cell phones, or chat rooms.

Cyber-bullying (also called online bullying) is willful, recurrent harm inflicted through the medium of electronic text; it's using the cyber world to harass through personal attacks or other means. One of the more recognized instances occurred when Eric Harris, one of the killers in the 1999 Columbine massacre, put up a Web site that discussed murdering fellow students. Another was "the Star Wars kid," whose classmates uploaded video of him posing as Darth Maul onto Kazaa in 2003. The footage was downloaded and modified extensively, causing him extensive embarrassment, resulting in psychiatric treatment and his dropping out of school. In 2005, *People* magazine noted that a thirteen-year-old boy had committed suicide after his classmates taunted and teased him about his size for a month via instant messaging.

# CYBER-BULLYING PREVENTION

**Things to Share With Your Kids**

▶ Never give out or share personal identification numbers (PINs) or share passwords with peers.

▶ Use Netiquette (Internet etiquette). Don't say things about others that you wouldn't want them to say about you.

▶ Don't send messages when angry; turn off the computer and walk away.

▶ If you encounter something online that doesn't look or feel right, it probably isn't.

▶ Don't reply to cyber-bullies. They want a rise out of you; don't give it to them.

**Ways to Help Your Kids**

▶ Keep your child's computer in a busy part of the house.

▶ Tell your child not to blame himself if he is victimized. And don't take the computer away (a big fear among kids) that won't end the problem.

▶ Create an Internet-Acceptable-Use Agreement with your child (Bullying.org has examples). They can help create a more civil and safe Internet society.

▶ Contact the police if you feel you need to.

▶ If a problem persists, do not delete or erase the messages. Print them out if possible. You might need the evidence later.

One national poll revealed that at least a third of teens have had mean, threatening, or embarrassing statements made about them online. In Illinois alone, researchers estimate that a half million kids have been victimized by cyber-bullying. Ten percent were threatened with physical harm (which is a crime). There's even software that allows people to text and instant message people as if they are someone else. There is no conventional way of tracking down the impostor. The anonymity allows bullies to be even more malicious.

Australia's Department of Education and Skills reported that one in five students have been victims of cyber-bullying. Yet one in three students never reported the incident.[9] Canada has taken a lead in this arena with tougher laws; under its Criminal Code, it is a crime to communicate repeatedly with someone if your communication causes them to fear for their own safety or the safety of others. It is also a crime to publish a "defamatory libel," writing something designed to insult a person or likely to hurt a person's reputation by exposing her to hatred, contempt, or ridicule.

# THE HORRIFYING IMPACT OF BULLYING

Hollywood actress Winona Ryder was speechless when she was asked for an autograph by a girl who beat her up in middle school. The crime? Wearing clothing from the Salvation Army, all she and her family could afford at the time. One day she got a hall pass so she could go to the bathroom. On her way, she was cursed, kicked, and had her head slammed against a locker. When she got up off the floor, she needed stitches.

Michelle Williams of Destiny's Child had trouble fitting in as well. She was ridiculed for being a good student, being skinny, being underdeveloped and not having boyfriends. Despite her woundedness, today she's thankful that God saw other qualities in her and chose her as His own.

Tom Cruise battled the effects of childhood abuse and bullies. He says his father, Thomas Cruise Mapother III, "was a bully and a coward . . . the kind of person who, if something goes wrong, they kick you. It was a great lesson in my life—how he'd lull you in, make you feel safe, and then, *bang!*"

Cruise struggled with anxiety at home *and* at school: "So many times the big bully comes up, pushes you. Your heart's pounding, you sweat, and you feel like you're going to vomit. . . . I don't like bullies."[10]

Patrick Swayze had to create a tough-guy image at an early age because of severe childhood persecution. He remembers being beat up since he was a small child. He recalls how it didn't matter that he was captain of the football team, gymnastic team, or that he did other sports—he was bashed anyway. He turned to martial arts to help him gain confidence and self-defense skills.

Even the pugnacious Bill O'Reilly, no lightweight when it comes to both size and personality, had to contend with bullies. He attended a private school on Long Island where male students had to wear a jacket and tie. His family didn't have as much money as other families, so his jackets "were cheap pieces of junk. . . . So a few wise guys started teasing me about my clothes." They pulled off his clip-on tie. They shoved him, cornered him at his locker, grabbed his jacket and mocked him. He says, "Bullying is inexcusable and no kid should have to put up with it."[11]

Thirteen-year-old Breanna Davis of Savannah, Georgia, says, "The first week they fought Alexis, the second week they jumped Devaree, the third week they jumped me." Her bruises have faded, but her consuming fear remains. Her crime? Sitting in the wrong part of the bus on the way home from school with her sister. A bully wanted her to move. She refused.

"He started screaming and spitting in my face and I still didn't do nothing. Then he smashed my head against the window!"

When she defended herself, other kids joined in and "beat me up, kicked me, boxed me—everything. The bus didn't stop. [The driver] kept going." The bullies then went out the emergency exit.[12]

Davis was sent to the hospital for a CAT scan. She's an A student, but who knows what effect bully-based trauma could have on her life. If or when her grades slip, will the two previous beatings she received in front of school employees be taken into consideration? Will anyone be held responsible?

For five months a thirteen-year-old New Zealand girl received abusive text messages, was pushed around at school, and avoided parts of school in fear for her own safety. Then she had to be escorted from her classroom by a teacher amid a barrage of name-calling.

The bullies didn't stop there. They called her at home and taunted her. She can't bring herself to go back to school and is so afraid that she is "camping" in her parents' bedroom (even though two teachers noticed her slipping confidence and apparent depression). She suffers from stress migraines and lack of sleep. Her mother laments, "I've complained so many times and seen my child being emotionally crippled. It takes all my might not to get out of the car and go over there" and batter those kids, she admits.

A New Zealand report stated that in general, schools failed to provide female students with enough protection. Worse, students who did seek support from schools "wound up more hurt and unhappy and lost respect for their teachers."[13]

Sixteen-year-old Jade Prest of England endured eighteen months of cyber-bullying. Her persecutors went so low as to portray her as a junkie. Midnight prank calls, an online chat room whispering campaign, abusive text messages, threats, intimidation, and the silent treatment became a way of life for Prest, who suffered from depression, eating disorders, panic attacks, and uncontrollable fear when her phone rang. She even considered suicide.

> The bullying affected me so deeply, we went to the police, the school, we did everything. My marks dropped, I gained a lot of weight, then lost too much. I retreated into myself. The worst thing I did was cut myself, but I was so out of it at that time.[14]

Her advice to other victims: "Tell someone, your parents, your teacher, anyone."

Kids are even resorting to free plastic surgery with the hope of stopping bullies from making fun of how they look. In Scotland alone, approximately six hundred in only five years have received free cosmetic surgery to keep bullies off their backs and out of their souls. Adam Searle, president of the British Association of Aesthetic Plastic Surgeons, said these children were under enormous strain. "With the media pressures on teenagers to look good, there may be an increase in requests for plastic surgery."[15]

In Glasgow, five teens had breast reductions. Nine had enlargements, and three had lifts. All seventeen young women, still developing, wanted their breasts to be carved with the hope that it would satisfy their bully's contentions that their appearances are so repulsive that they merit humiliation and scorn.

I have been staring at this fact for more than half an hour. Has the depth of the absurdity reached you yet? I'm not sure it's fully reached me. Imagine your daughter or sister being tormented about her forming chest for so long that a counselor has deemed her worthy of free surgery to banish perceived ugliness. Think of her at thirteen; imagine her undergoing knives, anesthesia, and breathing tubes, always with the risk of infection, to have her breasts altered in order to appease tormentors. She doesn't lie upon an operating table. She lies on an altar as a blood sacrifice of innocence and a capitulation to the grotesque cultural malady of bullying.

The demands of bullying proclaim: *You, girl, aren't worthy of basic human dignity the way you are. You must become unnatural.* Your daughter and your sister probably don't match up to the "standards" set by fashion and entertainment magazines and TV shows—the secret little sisters of porn. This is extortion by another name. Join me, please, in outrage.

# UNCOMFORTABLE TRUTH ABOUT VICTIMS

Like their tormentors, victims are misunderstood. Many think they get picked on because they wear glasses, are fat, have above-average grades, and so on. Though some children with these characteristics are bullied, many are not. The frustrating and painful truth goes deeper than spectacles, obesity, or ingenuity.

Here are characteristics that bind victims to isolation, humiliation, and despair:

- ▶ They acquiesce too quickly to demands.
- ▶ They cry and cower, sometimes making elaborate displays of pain and suffering, fueling further attacks.
- ▶ They offer too few healthy boundaries. They refuse to defend themselves, leaving their attackers undeterred to future attacks.
- ▶ Their lack of self-defense is noticed and disliked by both aggressive and non-aggressive peers.
- ▶ They don't take good-natured teasing well, mistaking it for outright criticism. They bristle easily and are short on humor.
- ▶ They often radiate low self-confidence with words, actions, and body language.

- ► They don't know how to join in and participate with their peers.

- ► They wear distress on their sleeves—they're socially not shrewd. They don't know how to conceal their feelings when doing so is wise and prudent.

- ► They often do not engage in sports and don't compete well when they do.

- ► They are more likely to have stomach pain, bed-wetting lapses, and fatigue. (The pain they feel is not just "in their head.")

- ► They are submissive *before* they're picked on.

This list was hard for me to study, consider, and accept when one of my children fell into the hands of a bullying crowd. Yet I did my child no favor, my anxious gut no favor, by pretending things didn't apply to my kid when they did. Those days are behind us now, but they wouldn't have been if we'd held on to our wounded pride and kept our heads in the sand instead of embracing a plan of action.

Parents of victims, please don't forget the study mentioned earlier where children who didn't know each other were put into groups in which bullies quickly found their victims. Recall how the victims refused to take a leadership role even when opportunities presented themselves. They spent their time in passive play, parallel to and apart from their peers rather than with them.

They are not embraced by their non-bullying peers *because* they are picked on. Kids, like adults, prefer smooth and worry-free relationships. The friction victims bring to school life is not wanted by other kids, even though the victim status is completely unfair. Most teachers are loath to admit that either bullying or victimization goes on, considering them an open indictment of their adequacy and supervision.

Isolation from their peers sets victims up for depression and anxiety during the pivotal adolescent years and beyond. This social marginalization is probably more damaging to them in the long run than the bullying itself. Worse, the maltreatment by both bullies and peers compels them not to trust others. They perceive themselves as incompetent in social situations and have a low view of their abilities. They underperform both professionally and personally.

If the list of victim characteristics reminds you of a previous chapter, it should. It reeks with the results of parental overprotection. Bully victims often come from overprotective homes where they get little if any practice handling conflict; as a result, they have little if any confidence in their ability to negotiate the world on their own. Overprotection prevents them from learning the skills necessary to avoid exploitation.

# DEADLY LESSONS

Taking matters into one's own hands can bring unforeseen consequences, like when Tianna Onyebuagum of Goodlettsville, Tennessee, told her son, Kenneth London, to strike back against his oppressor. He hit fifteen-year-old D'Angelo Karr with a rock and killed him. Onyebuagum received one-year of probation; her son will live the rest of his life with the memory of unjustifiable homicide.

Other parents have even become so fed up and angst-ridden that they've taken matters into *their* own hands, desperate and enraged after abdications of authority and a vacuum of common decency. Like Liang Jiqian, of China, a father sentenced to death for killing four boys and one woman and seriously injuring two other children. His son was continually bullied by local kids and villagers due to a bone disease that left the boy unable to speak or walk.

But it's the school shootings that hit us the hardest, as they should. Is there a place more important to communities than where their children gather to learn and socialize? A school shooting wounds us more as a community than a shooting inside a house of worship, than inside a court of law. Adults see schools as a tender place, a kind of greenhouse that cannot endure real-life elements too long without freezing or scorching what's inside. And that's our children, the focal point of so much worry and hope.

Our assumption is part of the problem. Those inside are not getting the protection they need. We can go ahead and blame "bad teachers" and self-serving school policies on bullying if it makes us feel better. But that will only make matters worse.

It's true, not every teacher should be teaching. And some studies show that an alarming number of teachers not only don't see clear incidents of bullying, but their lack of action when they do witness bullying is dismal.

However, what about a parent's inability to raise a child who would know inside that it's wrong to continually strip another person of common dignity? Isn't this where the problem begins? We're expecting *schools* to perform modern-day miracles. We're expecting *them* to reform children who receive inadequate parenting year after uninterrupted year. Teachers and administrators are not the root cause of this cultural problem, and it's not ultimately their task to correct it.

At Bethel Regional High School in Bethel, Alaska, on February 19, 1997, sophomore Evan Ramsey killed two people and wounded two others. It wasn't the school's fault. True, teachers either didn't know about the bullying or failed to act when they caught his fellow students calling him names. But other kids surely received similar treatment and didn't bring a gun to school to fulfill a bloodlust for revenge.

Ramsey's decline began with his parents, not his principal. His father, nicknamed the "Rambo of Alaska," was imprisoned when Ramsey was just seven; his mother slipped into the dark and selfish cave of alcoholism. Evan and his siblings were sent to foster homes, and in at least one he was sexually abused. He suffered from depression as young as ten and contemplated suicide when he was eleven.

More than twenty people knew Ramsey's plan to kill, but none came forward. One taught him how to use a shotgun, and one even brought a camera that day to capture the moments when he murdered Josh Palacios and principal Ron Edward, a former Marine whose wife, a substitute teacher, cradled him in her arms as he lay dying.

Ramsey put the loaded gun under his own chin but couldn't pull the trigger. In the hours after his killings, he said he felt "good," as if he had solved his problems. "Through my crime," he said, "I released hate and pain."[16]

Ramsey and two friends had compiled a mental hit list of teachers they hated and students who bullied them. Ramsey listed a ninth-grade girl and a boy among his chief bullies; they'd spit on him and called him stupid. "Nobody liked me, and I could never understand why," he said. He didn't shoot either one because he didn't see them.

He told the Secret Service he tried to get administrators to stop the bullying: "For a while they would go and talk to the person and tell them to leave me alone. But after a while, they just started telling me to ignore them." When asked why he acted out at school instead of elsewhere, Ramsey responded, "That's where most of my pain and suffering was. I figured since the principal and the dean weren't doing anything that was making any impression, that I was gonna have to do something, or else I was gonna keep on getting picked on."[17]

Ramsey wishes his two friends would have turned on him. "That would have been one of the best things a person could have done." Instead, his buddies egged him on. When asked, "If the principal had called you in and said, 'This is what I'm hearing,' what would you have said?" Ramsey replied, "I would have told him the truth." This he believes he would have said to the man he murdered.

Disillusioned youth identify with killers who went from victim to victimizer; their desire for revenge is formidable. Ramsey has a pen-pal fiancée. Kip Kinkel, serving a 112-year term for killing his parents and then two students in his Oregon high school in 1998, has received money in the mail from strangers. Charles Williams, in prison on charges of killing two students in Santee, California, gets more than forty letters a week; several different online clubs and homemade Web sites are dedicated to him. The Youth Violence Project devoted a portion of their Web sites to the following question: "My teenager saw all the news stories about the latest school shooting, and to my surprise, he said that the kids who did it were 'cool' and 'really brave.' What should I do?"[18]

After analyzing thirty-seven school shootings, the Secret Service found that "many of these children saw the killing as a way to solve a problem, such as to stop bullying by other children."[19] (That is to say, school shooters don't snap; they plan, often as they're haunted by depression and desperation.) The Service also warned against over-reliance on metal detectors, SWAT teams, profiles, zero-tolerance policies, and software. Researchers believe that

> [the answer] lies more in listening to children, dealing fairly with grievances such as bullying, improving the climate of communication in schools, keeping guns away from children, and investigating promptly and thoroughly when a student raises a concern.[20]

# HELP FOR ANGRY AND DESPERATE BOYS

Since the vast majority of kids who unleash this kind of violence are boys, here's a list of helpful tips for this kind of crisis. The following advice is from William S. Pollack, author of the bestselling *Real Boys and Real Boys' Voices,* assistant professor of psychology at Harvard Medical School, and consultant to the Secret Service on its study of school shootings. "The good news," he says, "is that when you can get boys to open up and talk to you, boys yearn to talk."[21]

► Honor a boy's need for "timed silence," to choose when to talk.

► Find a safe place, a "shame-free zone."

► Connect through activity and play. Many boys express their deepest experience through "action-talk."

► Avoid teasing and shaming.

► Make brief statements and wait; do not lecture.

► Share your own experiences (if relevant). It lets your boy know he is not alone with issues.

► Be quiet and really listen with complete attention.

► Convey how much you admire, care about, and love the boy.

► Give boys regular, undivided attention and listening space.

► Don't prematurely push him to be "independent."

► Encourage the expression of a full and wide range of emotions.

(continued)

- ▶ Let him know that real men do cry and do speak out.

- ▶ Express your love as openly as you might with a girl.

- ▶ When you see aggressive or angry behavior, look for the pain behind it.[22]
  Also:

- ▶ Protect him from sibling bullying whenever possible.

- ▶ Restrict access to movies and video games that carry with them themes of revenge and that glorify violence.

- ▶ The Secret Service reports that school shooters "told of behavior that, if they occurred in the workplace, would meet the legal definitions of harassment."[23] So take their concerns seriously. The report shows that bullying is not always a passage of adolescence but, for some, it's actual torture.

- ▶ Bullying creates in children a self-hatred. Look for overreactions to minor frustration, fear of new social situations, experimentation with drugs and alcohol, difficulty sleeping or eating, extreme isolation and withdrawal, chewing fingernails, inability to make friends, disinterest in school activities, and the bullying of others that didn't exist before.

- ▶ Children who are bullied may unexpectedly lash out at people or things around them, such as pets.

More than three-fourths of the killers were known to hold grievances, real or imagined, against the target and/or others. Two-thirds described feeling persecuted, bullied, or threatened—not teasing, but torment. In most cases, their retaliation was the first violent act against the target.

School killer Luke Woodham wrote in his journal: "I am not

insane. I am angry. I am not spoiled or lazy. . . . I killed because people like me are mistreated every day. . . . I am malicious because I am miserable."[24]

James Alan Kearbey, fourteen, murdered his principal and wounded three others in his junior high. He said he was bullied and beaten by students for years.

Nathan Faris, twelve, was harangued about his chubbiness. He shot a classmate, then killed himself.

John McMahan, fourteen, was bullied by other boys. He shot two students.

Joseph Todd, fourteen, shot two students who he said humiliated him.

This ledger of tragedy will continue until others—the estimated 85 percent who are neither bully nor victim—end their conspiracy of apathetic silence and confront bullying.

# MORE ADVICE FOR PARENTS

Barbara Coloroso, teacher and author in Littleton, Colorado, says she would handle her son's problems with bullies differently today.

> I took bullying seriously, but I didn't know how to deal with it effectively. My youngest child was targeted in grade school. . . . On top of it, he was a loudmouth, so his teacher didn't offer any help. Back then, we were livid, but we didn't know what to do. Now I'd go to the teachers and the other parents and make sure they dealt with the boys who were bullying my son. We would also work harder at helping him develop social skills, such as how to enter a group successfully. He was artistic and liked to do things by himself, but any small kid who is on the playground alone is an easy target. I wish I had worked harder to debunk the myth that bullying is normal.[25]

Coloroso reports that today her son is doing well as a professional artist.

Furthermore:

- Encourage your child to always tell you when she's being bullied (kids are prone to keep quiet).

- Demonstrate assertive behavior. Teach your children to ask for things directly and to respond directly to others. Demonstrate that it's okay to say no. Do so yourself, and let your kids see you doing it.

- Teach social skills. Show them how to resolve problems fairly and firmly.

- Identify potential friendship problems and correct them. Teach them how to ignore common teasing and, when possible, to respond with lighthearted humor. Teach them the value of friendship and the importance of being a good friend.

- Encourage them not to give in to bullies, to stand their ground with toys and territory.

- Demonstrate the rewards of personal achievement. Help them learn to trust their feelings so they can resist peer pressure and respect healthy adults. Help them set realistic goals, and let them work toward their goals without taking over the process yourself.

- *Take bullying seriously.*

# OUR CHOICE:
# BE PART OF THE AGONY,
# OR PART OF THE ANSWER

If you give one of these simple, childlike believers a hard time, bullying or taking advantage of their simple trust, you'll soon wish you hadn't. You'd be better off dropped in the middle of the lake with a millstone around your neck.

—Jesus (Mark 9:42 THE MESSAGE)

The last chapter addressed the main players on the stage of bullies and victims. Now it's time to turn our attention to the theater's audience. We tend to micro-focus on bullies and who they target without considering that most bullying wouldn't take place if not for the captive audience that both feeds a bully's ambitions and also sometimes becomes his accomplices.

They are the bystanders, the coat-holders who, by failing to act courageously, provide bullies their tacit approval. Again, by and large, victims are most children's second-least-favorite class-mates (after bullies). The bystanders don't yet realize, though, that coming to the aid of classmates is also a tangible act of self-pro-tection (from potential later violence). Worse, many of them actu-ally encourage tormentors to punch harder and longer, to write another humiliating line in an instant message, or to write one more rumor in a notebook.

This standby audience is also comprised of instructors, admin-istrators, Sunday school teachers, coaches—anyone who deals with youth and who, like me, have struggled to figure out what to do when one kid tramples another. As you'll note, our track record is pretty ugly.

# INNOCENT? BYSTANDERS?

When bullying occurs, where are the many children of faith? Statistically, they are absent. Or more accurately, given the clear moral foundations of major religions, they are missing in action. They are failing to defend the weak and confront injustice.

**MOST BULLYING WOULD NOT TAKE PLACE IF IT WEREN'T FOR THE DISPLAY OF POWER THEY WANT OTHERS TO WITNESS.**

Where are the millions of adults who read *The Purpose-Driven Life*? Why don't they contribute their strength and protection to bully victims? Did they skip over Day 20 of the book? "Peacemaking is not *avoiding conflict*. Running from a problem, pretending it doesn't exist, or being afraid to talk about it is actually cowardice. Jesus, the Prince of Peace, was never afraid of conflict. On occasion he *provoked* it for the good of every-one. . . . Peacemaking is not *appeasement*. Always giving in, acting like a doormat, and allowing others to run over you is not what Jesus had in mind." (Day 20, *The Purpose-Driven Life,* 153.) As we'll see, they're missing in action because so many people of faith think it's wrong to do conflict. Being bold and courageous on behalf of others is not part of their spiritual training.

Remember that about 85 percent of all school-based bullying takes place in front of other kids—that gives bullies the emotional high and ego stroke they're seeking. *Most bullying would not take place if it weren't for the display of power they want others to witness.*

Bystanders vastly outnumber both predators and prey. Yet once more, research shows that most do not intervene. This is particularly unfortunate because, according to Focus on the Family, school "policies encouraging bystanders to get involved when a child is being bullied—either by standing up for the child or by telling an adult—have proved to be effective."[1]

The reason for their lack of intervention comes down to basic human nature. The indifferent, confused, and/or fearful masses who witness bullying are urged from within not to be courageous and protective but to shrink instead. In all my research regarding what bullying does to kids, not one group or facility has tried to quantify how cowardice impacts bystanders. This remains one of the most under-examined and probably damaging aspects of bullying.

Not only do the masses fail to stand up for those who need help, they too often give into a depraved temptation to join the bully in the quest for humiliation.

In a binder called a "Slam Book" that circulated in a Toronto classroom (these make the rounds in U.S. schools also), each page bore a malicious heading: Who's the Stupidest. Who's the Ugliest. Who's the Most Unpopular (and so on). Almost all the girls in the class nominated another person, which had a heavy impact on the kids being named. Most of these girls were really "nice" kids, which again highlights a major point: Nice does not equal good.

Eight of the ten students involved would never have taken part in publicly humiliating their fellow students on their own.

Because of peer pressure, the temptation to make another look and feel smaller than them, and the lockstep importance of belonging to a group, they engaged in immense cruelty. Like most children (including churchgoers) when it comes to bullying, they lacked the ability to do the right thing when others were doing wrong. They lacked moral courage.

According to the Secret Service study of school shootings,

> Those who knew in advance sometimes encouraged the attack and sometimes urged an escalation of the plan, but only rarely told anyone or shared their concern with others before the attack. In about one-third of the cases, the attack was influenced or dared by others or a group.[2]

These cannot be described as "innocent bystanders," one of our language's most ironic euphemisms.

# TEACHERS GET LOW GRADES

Public schools frequently receive unfair criticism, some of which is outright wrong and some even on the level of a hoax. For example, you may have heard about a survey that supposedly compared the major concerns of teachers in 1940 with those at the end of the century. The 1940 list included, for example, talking, chewing gum, and running in the halls; contemporary concerns were drug abuse, pregnancy, suicide, assault, and so on. This "survey" appeared in magazines like *Time* and *Newsweek* and newspapers such as the *New York Times* and the *Wall Street Journal*.

When Barry O'Neill, a professor at Yale University, investigated the origins, he collected more than 250 different versions of the claimed surveys and eventually traced them to T. Cullen Davis of Fort Worth, Texas. Asked how he arrived at the lists, Davis told O'Neill, "They weren't done from a scientific survey. How did I know what the offenses in the schools were in 1940? I was there.

How do I know what they are now? I read the newspapers."[3] Although the lists were exposed as a hoax in 1994, they continue to be cited as factual.

As already mentioned, public schools are unfairly expected to clean up after our culture's abdication of parental responsibility, which is endemic. Yet studies also show that when it comes to bullying, school officials are nowhere near as alert and proactive as they like to believe.

Dr. Debra Peplar documented more than four hundred episodes of bullying at public schools, lasting an average of thirty-seven seconds. Teachers noticed and intervened in a paltry one out of twenty-five episodes.

In a similar study, 91 percent of teachers who admitted there was bullying in their classrooms dismissed it as minor. One-fourth confided that it was helpful sometimes just to ignore bullying. A study of victimized children in Norway confirmed that teachers seldom take action; up to 60 percent of victims reported that teachers rarely, or never, put a stop to bullying.[4] In Canada, Peplar found that only 35 percent of students reported teacher intervention, yet 85 percent of teachers insist that they intervene nearly always or often.

Do you see why students are afraid to speak up? They perceive adults as uncaring or unable to provide protection. They are witnesses to the well-documented tendency of teachers to underestimate the prevalence and severity of bullying and to ignore it when it occurs. "Who, after all, is going to take the solitary word of a child demeaned by peers, disregarded by teachers, and possibly also by parents?"[5] Especially parents who overemphasize compliance in their kids? As these children already have no real allies among their peers, it's safe to conclude that many of them believe that God doesn't care about them either. Why would He, if no one else does?

In one amazing thirty-seven-minute episode where a child

was repeatedly kicked and thrown around by two kids, the victim was willing. "What's so strange to me," complains Peplar, "is that he stays in it. There are lots of opportunities for him to get away. At one point a teacher even approaches and tries to break it up, and all three of them say, 'Oh no, we're just having fun.'"[6] Experts say one possible explanation is that victimhood is better than anonymity; that is, for some, being picked on is preferable to not being noticed.

Just how much can we expect a teacher or school employee to protect a child who is unwilling to even try to protect himself? We as a society cannot expect teachers to make up for such a severe lack of self-respect. The responsibility for such faulty thinking rests with parents.

Regarding teachers' failure to intervene, some complain to journalists that they worry about legal repercussions from out-of-control parents who create bullies. As a coach, I've had to contend with this as well; one mother threatened to sue me when I dealt with her bully boy. I felt sorry for the teachers unfortunate enough to have him in their class.

But I think the main reason teachers and administrators often don't notice bullying is entirely straightforward: they witness so much of it that they become desensitized. Authority often sees the shadow of bullying but not the act itself. What I usually see or hear when bullying is going down is an out-of-place body movement, an oddly timed snicker, a strange facial expression. I often don't see or hear the actual thing—I see or hear its ill-defined consequences. I see a kid in pain but don't know for sure its source. I possess no solid proof. And he's not likely to talk about it when I do follow my intuition and ask questions. It can take well over half an hour to get to the bottom of the issue, to put enough pressure on a team to find out what really happened. And, like a teacher, I don't have thirty minutes to spend.

## IDEAS FOR SCHOOLS

Schools in England are providing online surveys for students, asking them to name bullies and give specific information about their behavior. The information goes to select staff members. Initial reports suggest this innovative approach is helping to break the intimidation factor that stops many children from telling authorities what they know.

Some of these schools also have dramatically reduced bullying and vandalism by replacing communal bathrooms with single bathrooms attached to or just outside classrooms. Another school is considering a kind of zero-tolerance policy for bullying where detention, minimally, is mandatory for each abuse.

Children in Edinburgh, Scotland, are encouraged to report bullies by text message into a confidential database. The information is analyzed for patterns of behavior, and kids are getting over their fear of speaking out. Cyber-bullying, meet cyber-self-defense.

# THE STORY OF MY OWN BULLY TRANSFORMATION

It can be difficult to find empathy and affection for victims. As stated previously, they can be painfully non-assertive. They bristle easily. They're often out of step with their peers because timidity robs them of spontaneity. They sometimes don't get jokes because they're so guarded and self-focused. They require a lot of what coaches call baby-sitting. Their inability to acclimate is so stark that sometimes we feel we can only erect a kind of fence around them. Soccer is a contact sport (as is school), so this fence almost never works.

And I just scratch my head regarding their parents.

I wonder, *Why didn't they warn me about this? Why didn't they tell me ahead of time so we could come up with a plan? Do they think I'm a miracle worker?*

It's parents who almost always make a good coach hang up his whistle. I've already spoken of bully parents; victim parents often say nothing about their child's inability to get along with other kids, then turn around and blame the coach for not ensuring his complete emotional safety. Coaches can't do this any more than teachers can—and if we could, doing so would only turn victims into pariahs. Why aren't the parents themselves stepping up? If a child cannot integrate outside of the home, the origin of the problem is rarely the school or the field; it's usually the home itself.

As to the rare moments where I've witnessed clear examples of bullying, there exists inside me what I'm ashamed to call my inner Lord of the Flies. I've been tempted, especially as a younger coach, to join in—to turn the knife of verbal taunting, to quench the youthful fire in the victim's eyes. To make him suffer, to see him feel the shot, to take perverse pleasure in destruction.

Even then, this lust didn't happen often. I suspect that, like an urge toward adultery, it rises when my soul is weakened and needy for power and pleasure at any price.

With this temptation comes an inner war.

"Say it!" yells a loud, obnoxious voice, full of confidence and swagger. "Cut him down!"

"Defend him," says a quiet and noble voice. "Correct this situation."

I've searched my memory to see if I've ever given in to such a temptation. I don't believe I have. I hope I haven't. If I have, I pray God will forgive me.

That's what extreme displays of weakness and non-assertive-ness can do to people—make them want to join in and bully too. Honest and introspective counselors notice this tendency and are mindful in dealing with it. In many ways, defending a picked-on kid is in accordance with our conscience, but not in accord with a darker part of us, the bully within most everyone. It's vital that leaders acknowledge this temptation and actively oppose it.

It would be disingenuous of me to write about bullying's dev-astation without searching my own soul and telling you about my season as a bully. My bullying life started in junior high and hit its zenith in high school. Sarcasm was my best and often only weapon. I could not be bested. I used my gift for seeing irony, hypocrisy, and weakness in others and unleashed my observations. I did it to people who had what I wanted: girlfriend, clothing, car. I could dismantle them with a sentence, leaving them stripped, defenseless, resentful, and sometimes furious.

Like most bullies, I attacked those I knew I could beat. I don't believe I shot my venom into anyone I thought was smarter than me. I was a coward.

I got this talent from my mother, a funny and smart woman. She had a powerful sense of humor, wicked at times. I inherited the ability to leave an opponent speechless before a crowd. I could leave an insult lingering in the air like potpourri. I could place a joke on a person who wouldn't understand it for minutes, while everyone else got it sooner, making him look like a dunce.

I could meet a person for the first time, read him, and then use my insight against him. If he was uncomfortable, I caught on quickly. If he said something that needed further support, I pointed it out. If he couldn't defend it, I pointed that out too, usually with barbed sarcasm, making myself look (or at least feel) powerful and smart.

I even did this to my friends. One grew weary of it and punched me so hard my children should have been born with a headache. I left him alone after that. More people should have punched me—that was the only boundary I respected. Pain with a message is hard to ignore.

Even though I still remember that punch, it wasn't until my early twenties that I could see what I was doing to others. The friendships I strained and even lost. The glares I got from people unfortunate enough to draw too close to me at parties and who set off in me the desire to take them down a notch, even without cause.

Gradually some mental clouds began to part. I gained a better understanding of my own unhappiness, which was more vast and jagged than I assumed, and I could see rays of light into what I was really doing. I'd experienced God's love by then. I was blessed by His presence and His good intent for me, and so I wanted to do something better with what He'd given me. I wanted to be a redemptive force, though I wasn't sure how.

I repented.

I decided to lay off people. I decided I would hold my tongue and not make the witty statement I knew would get a laugh but would also cast a pall over someone and keep the conversation on edge. Instead I would try to speak words that edified, which I hate to admit was uncomfortable at first. It takes a certain kind of power and clarity to bless another. I had the desire to do this, but I wasn't sure about my ability to pull it off. I had to work hard at it—being good requires more than a nice desire. I needed strength, insight, and a level of comfort with risk that I didn't have.

I wanted to be better to people, and with time I learned how. I met people who blessed others in this way, most notably a good man named Craig Black, and I tried to emulate his behavior. I had to fight the temptation to pierce another's dignity, which usually happened when I felt uncomfortable, scared, or weak. I suspect this is similar to the temptation all recovering bullies must fight.

There's another reason I wanted to change, and I wish it were noble by way of motive, but it's not. I grew tired of hurting people. Shredding souls lost its allure. So what if I could dim the light in someone's eyes? I'd seen it so many times it was beginning to make me feel sick inside. It was also around this time that I started thinking more about other people's troubles. I had some that wouldn't go away—for instance, heartaches that persisted for years without apparent relief. My own troubles were so pervasive that I made a sort of truce with them, and my inability to shed them began to give me multihued empathy and compassion for others as I considered them.

To this day, I avoid publications known for their jadedness (*Rolling Stone* comes to mind). They awaken and produce a primal sap in me to turn people into thin replicas of their true selves so I can feel the pleasure of knocking them down. This is akin to the deception of fantasy relationships and pornography.

I still firmly believe in the power of sarcasm and the truth it can proclaim. Sarcasm, if handled rightly, can be a redemptive force for good. But it's a difficult handling to pull off. It's hard to keep your ego out of it and instead wield the sword of humor on behalf of everyone's well-being, which is part of the definition of righteousness. Today, I try to reserve sarcasm for pointing out universal, corporate, or mutual hypocrisy. When I'm really brave and courageous, I turn my sarcasm upon myself.

I am a prodigal bully, a guy who realized the error of my ways in frustrating sputters and who later obtained the desire to protect kids from bullies like my former self. I've retained my ability for outrage, which can bring problems within the church, since nice people don't do outrage.

There's plenty of opportunity to take on bullying when you work with kids. Among the best ways is to be proactive. Go after it before it gets a chance at a foothold in the group you serve. Being proactive is so critical because of how much occurs away from the somewhat cataract-inhibited eyes of authority. You deal with the influence of bullying far more often than with its clearest forms, so like a gardener who lightly tills the soil before weeds form, address this common enemy before it has a chance to take root and become strong.

For example, I took over a soccer program known for hazing freshmen. Hazing is the kiss of death to a team, primarily because it kills teamwork and puts young minds into perpetual stress and fear where they can't learn. For the life of me I don't see why a coach tolerates hazing. What kid wants to sweat alongside another kid who's been giving him a hard time for no reason other than that he can abuse power and a coach lets him? How is such a kid going to feel valuable to a program?

During my first talk to the team I announced with force that there would be no hazing. I'm not exaggerating when I tell you that a chorus of thank-you's came from the freshmen while stretching. They too knew of the soccer program's reputation for hazing. It was in their minds even on the first day.

Dr. James Dobson, as a teacher, said something similar.

> I made it clear to my students that I wouldn't put up with teasing. . . . When a strong, loving teacher comes to the aid of the least-respected child in the class, something dramatic occurs in the emotional climate of the room. Every child seems to utter an audible sigh of relief. The same thought bounces around in many little heads: If that kid is safe from ridicule, then I must be safe, too.[7]

Now, here's the remarkable thing. Many of the seniors expressed relief as well. It's as if they wanted permission to be different than the seniors who went before them. As if they would be seen as being weak if they didn't haze, that they would lose face with their peers if they didn't abuse their power and influence.

I was scared to be courageous in this way. A coach knows he needs to be viewed by players in at least a somewhat likeable light. You don't need to be their best friend, which isn't good, but you don't want to earn their ire too early, too often. I put on a brave face. I spoke loudly and with as few words as possible. I intended to take a chance for the betterment of everyone. I forced myself to become a protector.

## COURAGE IS NOT OPTIONAL!

You don't have to go to a house of worship to know right from wrong. But we expect something more, don't we, from people who know God's commands to confront injustice? Yet year after year I am sorely disappointed by the cowardly behavior of kids who belong to God and know He desires that His people defend the weak. These children need to be inspired and empowered to do exactly that.

If you doubt this observation, put it to the test. Read your children's Sunday school or youth group curriculum. Go back as many years as you can. Volunteer in their classes and observe what they're being told. Ask them what they talked about and learned. You'll discover this: *Churchgoing kids are instructed nearly exclusively on how to avoid sin.* Their spiritual training consists of what a person shouldn't do. Avoiding sin is good and right. But what they're missing, what our culture is missing, is full and consistent instruction about what *to* do—which includes standing up for those being abused.

We want our children to stay away from sins of commission—choices and actions that are wrong. Yet we're not also teaching them the consequences that come from the sins of omission: *not* making choices and *not* doing acts that are right. Yes, it's good when they avoid doing wrong. But what about when they avoid doing right? Sometimes it's what they don't do that facilitates disharmony and decay in the world. *When we fail to love, we sin.*

**MANY SUNDAY SCHOOL CURRICULA DON'T EVEN INCLUDE COURAGE AS FUNDAMENTAL TO A VIRTUOUS LIFE.**

Many Sunday school curricula don't even include courage as fundamental to a virtuous life. Some teachers relegate courage to the personal realm, telling children they need to exercise the courage to say no to others. That's important. But it entirely misses the Bible's admonishment to say no on behalf of others.

Christians are encouraged to feed and clothe the needy, and this is excellent. But we're rarely challenged to *defend* those in need. Why the distinction? Because helping the poor usually doesn't include conflict; defending the needy often does. We don't like conflict, so we ignore this side of our faith life, yet we'll never attain a purpose-driven life if we don't learn how to do conflict well. And until we do, the weak will continue to suffer.

I explained in *No More Christian Nice Guy* how being nice instead of good ruins individual lives. My wife and I showed in *Married . . . But Not Engaged* how being nice instead of good ruins families. Now I'm demonstrating that being nice instead of good about bullying shreds souls and abdicates our responsibilities to the most needy among us. Bullying burns a child's psychological skin; how can we imagine that it's "unchristian" to put out the fire?

Good people stand up to injustice. Nice people don't—they

slink away and cover their cowardly tracks. Good people make enemies for the right reasons—Jesus wouldn't have told us to pray for our enemies if He thought we wouldn't make any. Nice people worry too much about the approval of others to make an enemy when they should; they go with the crowd, right or wrong.

Niceness is often a disguise for indifference and apathy. With time, with enough failed opportunities to forge moral courage, goodness, and righteousness, *the reward many nice people receive is that everyone likes them—except themselves and those who depend on them for protection and provision.* A nice person is usually an appeaser, one who, as Sir Winston Churchill said, "feeds a crocodile, hoping it will eat him last." An appeaser is willing to overlook injustice in order to be liked by those who desperately need correction; he worships the quicksand they walk on.

Christians talk about the Culture War. But how many are Culture Warriors? Worst of all, many who *do* take up this redemptive work are quickly criticized for "not doing it right" . . . by those too cowardly to venture outside their lives of excess and comfort . . . those who can't even bring themselves to protect children.

And even worse, many believers contend that it would be wrong to verbally or physically confront others in order to help the timid and defend the weak. Christians, sadly, need permission to be morally courageous again, as when they battled to abolish slavery, as when they have warred against expanding fascism, for minorities' basic civil rights, and for unborn children. *People of faith need permission to be good again—permission to exercise moral courage in civic life.*

# BAD "CHRISTIAN" ADVICE

On my radio talk show, when I've talked about bullying and our need to protect children from it, I've received adamant calls

NO MORE JELLYFISH, CHICKENS, OR WIMPS

from believers who say we should *not* confront such behavior. If a child suffers, it's God's will she suffer, they allege. If a kid suffers at the hands of a bully, then God is teaching him patience and humility—he's being persecuted for righteousness' sake. The facts say otherwise, and the children these people influence are getting terrible advice.

I got some of this as a young adult. I once worked for a wicked bully who abused with his body and his mouth (though he was ever so careful not to do or say anything illegal—at least nothing you could prove without recorded conversations or access to vital records). Like many bullies, he invaded physical boundaries, that hula-hoop-like space around each one of us, approximately the length of your arm in all directions from your center. He invaded intentionally, when it was to his advantage. I could see the look of satisfaction in his eyes when he stepped into another's unspoken area—not illegally, just unethically. I'd watch the other person back up in discomfort as the boss moved in, winning the negotiation advantage through physical intimidation.

He was a gifted twister of words. He knew just how far he could falsely state and falsely accuse without too much backlash. He measured people's tolerance, then exploited it. When you did defend yourself, he'd question your loyalty and spirituality. He only backed down to someone who threatened to use more force than he was willing to use, a brute who only respected power. He devoured and exploited the precious social grace that people extend to one another (this is a form of infidelity), consuming it and turning it into a paycheck.

Making matters worse was his practice of hiring a certain kind of Christian: the gentle-Jesus-meek-and-mild variety. The kind who's easily led, manipulated, and not trained to stand up to wrongdoing. The kind who thinks it's wrong to erect healthy boundaries. The kind who's already often psychologically damaged and so is ripe for exploitation. The kind who too easily follows the mandates of authority, even when corrupt. The kind who will not confront wickedness because he's been taught that he shouldn't.

Being around this man for eight-plus hours a day felt like being molested while half awake. You knew it was real, but you didn't have sufficient evidence to prove it. He had the ability to make you think you were going crazy. His smile often lacked authenticity but frequently was still able to charm. When he smiled, it gave you the creeps because you knew something wasn't right.

Seeking spiritual guidance on how to deal with this man was among the biggest mistakes I've ever made. Let me back up: It's wise to seek spiritual guidance, but make sure the people you seek it from actually possess wisdom.

I received unanimous "guidance." The reason I was at that job? God was trying to teach me patience and humility. Sound familiar? What's interesting is that I wasn't known for being too impatient or arrogant—in fact I was already patient to a fault. Yet this was the spiritual direction I received, given with amazing confidence, so I acted upon it with a blazing naïveté of my own. When you are naïve and too trusting, you're unable to guard your heart, a wellspring of life (Proverbs 4:23).

I was told just to wait: "The Holy Spirit is going do a mighty work" in this man's heart. "Just give it time. Pray for him and get out of the way." I did all this with the devotion of a medieval monk. If the Holy Spirit did correct him, it never showed. He got worse. Most in the office and many outside knew he was out of control, yet no one intervened. I watched people with sparkling church reputations pretend they saw nothing wrong. Their cowardly nature was mistaken for virtue; it was self-interest disguised as stoicism and faithfulness.

For my part, I kept waiting. Waiting for the Lord to teach me more patience with being abused, and waiting for my good behavior to bring about a transformation in my boss. What I saw instead was a fiend take even greater advantage of others who continued to lie down and roll over in the name of being Christians. I saw the powerful abuse the weak. I saw people break apart, become disillusioned and frail. I saw co-workers plunge into despair. I saw rashes break out on skin. I saw staff members attack each other like rats in an experiment. I heard people yelling at their spouses on the phone, people who didn't do this before. I witnessed sin loosening its tether and expanding its territory without resistance. I learned to tolerate wickedness. I heard people curse God.

I learned to lie to my soul, to live with evil instead of denouncing it when I saw the perverse pleasure the boss received by playing with people's lives like a cat with mice. Common human sin and its clear consequences were so highly spiritualized that the environment no longer had contact with reality. Wickedness wasn't wicked, not really; it was goodness in the making, I was told. Though I believe in redemption, that good can come from bad, my experience is that it doesn't happen automatically or inexorably. Believing good is emerging from evil, when it isn't, can make people accomplices to wickedness.

I learned to pretend I didn't feel angry or humiliated. When I did admit I felt this way, I was told I was wrong to complain or feel injured—this was God's way of beating pride out of me, so "consider it all joy." God ordained my misery, and He did not want me to exert my will in self-defense, which would cut short His education for me. This was a devastating parcel of guidance considering I was far more prone to self-doubt than self-promotion. Self-doubt and self-loathing escalated.

I allowed myself to be plundered with well-intentioned foolishness. I wrestled for years with my resultant wounded spirit, which was partly self-inflicted by my own negligence to defend myself. I labored to drain a small lake of resentment inside me, hard to do without stopping the inflow of abuse through healthy boundaries.

Even more remarkable is that I later had a business dealing with one of my erstwhile "spiritual" advisors who, with great charisma and confidence, had advocated a non-assertive approach toward my problem. This man who advised patience and humility in suffering was as ruthless as any secular CEO. He made sure no one ever got the better of him. Suffering, apparently, was what *other* people were born to experience. "Do as I say, not as I do." You know the story.

I hope it's obvious why I'm sharing all this. I suffered at the hands of a bully because of foolish advice I received that sounded pious and virtuous. What I was told to do, today's bully-victims are told to do.

## I WAS TOLD TO LAY DOWN MY WORTH BECAUSE IT WAS "WORLDLY" TO RETAIN IT.

Like school kids, I didn't suffer because of my faith or for righteousness but because others knew they could take advantage of an uneven playing field. I didn't suffer because of my beliefs. I suffered because it was to someone else's advantage to strip me. I suffered because in his mind my dignity was expendable, convertible into currency, or as on a school ground, a good laugh or display of power. I was told to lay down my worth because it was "worldly" to retain it. This man possessed excessive self-esteem, yet I was told the real problem God was trying to correct was *my* inflated self-esteem.

I have since seen how truly successful and virtuous people do not listen to such spiritualized stupidity. They are crafty, shrewd, boundary-setting people. I would come to see this in better bosses and colleagues.

# TURN YOUR CHEEK?

There is no greater argument within the community that promotes not standing up to injustice and freedom-crushing than Jesus' much-quoted (and torturously ill-applied) statement that "if someone strikes you on the cheek, offer the other also" (Luke 6:29 NRSV).

Countless churches have taken this to mean that Christians, especially Christian children, are to adopt a fully passive approach to the outside world, including bullying. We're not to push back. We're to acquiesce.

The first angle to address is hypocrisy. Most such parents would not allow themselves to be treated in the workplace the way they tell their children to allow themselves to be treated when bullied. They're expecting their children to undergo an environment they themselves are unwilling to face. In this way they are like the Pharisees Jesus chastised.

But someone not living up to a principle doesn't make the principle flawed. Let me take this to another level. According to the perspective adopted by many Christians, there are few if any exceptions to this statement of Jesus. In their home, then, if a child strikes a parent on the face, that parent (according to his interpretation of the text) is required to do more than not resist. That parent *also* must not correct such behavior. If there aren't exceptions, then there aren't exceptions. After all, Jesus never said He allowed for the exception of children striking parents.

We all know that healthy parenting is based in part upon a line of respect regarding a parent's authority. A myopic interpretation of Luke 6:29 destroys this line of respect and with it the ability to parent well. This is what happens when we overemphasize one verse/passage of God's Word at the expense of others, or when we refuse to consider His full counsel, or when we force our inclinations into the context of Scripture.

If defending yourself after being struck on the face is wrong or even sinful, then Jesus was wrong. Worse, Jesus sinned.

Meanwhile, the high priest questioned Jesus about his disciples and his teaching.

"I have spoken openly to the world," Jesus replied. "I always taught in synagogues or at the temple, where all the Jews come together. I said nothing in secret. Why question me? Ask those who heard me. Surely they know what I said."

When Jesus said this, one of the officials nearby struck him in the face. "Is this the way you answer the high priest?" he demanded.

"If I said something wrong," Jesus replied, "testify as to what is wrong. But if I spoke the truth, why did you strike me?" (John 18:19–23).

The first admonishment (Luke 6:29) is not intended to adopt passivity in response to abuse. Jesus pushes back by appealing to a general assumption that people should be treated with a common level of respect and decency. When this social contract is broken, as it is with bullying, we are free to protest and require amends. It should also be pointed out that Jesus used physical force when He cleared the temple of the money-changers, after witnessing clear examples of abuse of authority and power. Not only did He overturn tables, He made a whip with His own hands in a premeditated act of justice and righteousness.

So does Jesus contradict himself? Not at all, when we take His statement in context.

Jesus' statement about turning our cheek most plainly applies to retaliation, and His command is clear: Don't do it. Jesus did not retaliate by returning blow for blow, insult for insult. But He did protest with words and with physical intimidation. This more sane and healthy view was promoted by C. S. Lewis in "Why I Am Not a Pacifist":

I think the text means exactly what it says, but with an understood reservation in favour of those obviously exceptional cases which every hearer would naturally assume to be exceptions without being told. . . . That is insofar as the only relevant factors in the case are an injury to me by my neighbour and a desire on my part to retaliate, then I hold that Christianity commands the absolute mortification of that desire. *No quarter whatever is given to the voice within us which says, "He's done it to me, so I'll do the same to him."*[8]

Perhaps people who use Scripture to contend that we should never defend ourselves from or protest foul treatment should call themselves passi-thiests. Their doctrine, which isn't biblically supported, fosters a passive and victimizing approach toward life, for themselves *and* for others (remember Jesus' statement about children and millstones?).

On October 2, 2006, Charles Carl Roberts IV, a milk-truck driver, entered the one-room West Nickel Mines School in Bart Township, Pennsylvania, with a handgun, a shotgun, a bolt-action rifle, about six hundred rounds of ammunition, cans of black powder, a stun gun, two knives, a change of clothes, and a box containing a hammer, hacksaw, pliers, wire, screws, bolts, and tape. He barricaded the school doors before binding the Amish hostages' arms and legs. He ordered them to line up against the chalkboard and released the fifteen male students, along with a pregnant woman and three parents with infants. The remaining ten female students he kept inside. The teacher contacted the police upon escaping by using a neighbor's phone; the first officers arrived within ten minutes and tried (unsuccessfully) to communicate with Roberts.

Police broke through the windows when shots were heard. The gunman apparently killed five girls and himself. Three of the girls died at the scene, two more the next morning from related injuries. They were shot execution-style, in the head. Their ages ranged from six to thirteen. It's likely more would have been killed if not for the bravery of the police, who thankfully possessed and used lethal force. Praise God that this calamity wasn't even worse.

How can a person abhor the use of deadly force in his own hands but not hesitate to call 9-1-1 in order to bring deadly force to the door when needed? If someone believes it's morally reprehensible to use deadly force, why is it not sinful either to have it used on his own behalf or to have it used for others at his behest? Such thinking reminds me of legalistic people who will not work on Sunday but who go after Sunday service to restaurants where an entire crew works to feed them. If it's wrong to work on the Sabbath, why make others work? It's wrong to perpetuate transgression, just as it's wrong to transgress.

*Self-defense and proper self-regard do not equate retaliation.* They do not represent eye for eye, tooth for tooth. Their aim is not revenge but rather to keep boundaries established and clear, and when possible to protect from harm. Many of the Ten Commandments are based upon the foundational premise that sin between humans has at its base the violation of one by another. If one does not hold firmly to right boundaries, one facilitates sin and its subsequent horrors.

I learned a lot from my workplace bullying experience. It shaped my thoughts about what happens to our children when they receive similar treatment. It gave me the ability to tell their story for them. And, equally important, I experienced what happens inside a person who fails to respond well to the challenge.

Looking back, I now believe that what God was trying to teach me, the virtue He wanted me to exercise and grow, was moral courage (not patience) in the face of wickedness. Of course patience is an incredible virtue—who couldn't use more of it in his life? But the same argument can be and should be made for courage.

Who even talks about moral courage today? Spiritual growth, especially courage, is fed by what we do in community. It's faith in action, discernable by others and yourself. Remember, the Bible says the righteous are as bold as lions; right now, we think the righteous are as soft as marshmallows. I'm going with the Word; I hope you do too.

And I hope you agree by now that standing up to the injustice of bullying is the Christian thing to do. People of a faith that promotes justice for all must take the lead tackling mistreatment—in this case, school-based abuse. Read on to hear about a movement I've started to help us do this.

# THE PROTECTORS: LETTING FAITH GET IN THE WAY

You may be 38 years old, as I happen to be. And one day, some great opportunity stands before you and calls you to stand up for some great principle, some great issue, some great cause. And you refuse to do it because you are afraid . . . that you will lose your job, or you're afraid that you will be criticized or that you will lose your popularity. . . . Well you may go on and live until you are 90, but you're just as dead at 38 as you would be at 90. And the cessation of breathing in your life is but the belated announcement of an earlier death of the spirit.

—Martin Luther King Jr.[1]

*A wounded spirit.* That's how I described my inner life after being bullied as an adult, and it's a term used by bestselling author Frank Peretti to describe his torturous experience at the hands of school bullies. He writes, "A bruise or a cut is visible, but a wounded spirit can remain buried deep inside a person unless you provide the environment that will bring it out and heal it."[2]

Cruelty is a destruction George Bernard Shaw saw as possessing inherent evil: "To break a man's spirit is the devil's work."

Peretti's personal account was shared on a *Focus on the Family* broadcast in October 1999. Focus then received more than 3,000 telephone calls, surprising both Peretti and staff members. The topic clearly resonated.

In a private conversation with Dr. James Dobson before being his radio guest, I commended him and Focus for being the only faith organization in my awareness to regularly speak out against school-based bullying. Dobson leaned back in his chair and accepted my compliment with warmth and humility. Then he told me about a huge regret from his childhood. One of those moments you wish you could take back. A moment your conscience won't let you forget.

He called a classmate "Jeep ears," because the ears stuck out so much they resembled large fenders. The young James thought it was a funny remark, sure to get a laugh. But "the boy heard what I said and was so hurt that he ran out of the room." Dobson doesn't remember the kid coming back, and his face, sixty-some years later, still showed remorse. "The teacher should have pulled me aside and made me apologize to that young man. She should have protected that boy."

## WITH TIME, MANY BULLIES *AND* THEIR TARGETS REGRET THE WHOLE ORDEAL.

With time, many bullies *and* their targets regret the whole ordeal. They wish they could grab the big hand of life's clock and turn it back. Like my friend, now in his fifties, who grew up in a devout Christian community where church attendance was obligatory. "I was teased throughout my school years for being overweight." He still battles his weight and his emotions, and perhaps he always will.

His eyes water when he recounts feeling humiliated and small, shaking with fear and anger before his tormentors. Feeling like no one, nowhere, so scared his bladder was ready to empty itself all over him. Forming a small, tight fist yet keeping it sheathed at his side, knowing it would do no good against his more powerful oppressors. Having his young mind filled with rage and receiving no tangible help—being told to "just ignore them," the most common piece of worthless advice in "protecting" a child's young spirit from harm. The paint on his house of horrors just won't dry. It still colors his future in ways only God really knows. He's a warm, loving, yet wounded man today. I care about him deeply.

Like many victims, he can't remember one child in his community who tried to help. He was publicly ridiculed off and on for fourteen years, and the public was mute. A public of children and adults who went to church and Sunday school yet didn't say even the one crisp word all knew since toddlerhood: "Stop!" Children who knew inside their God-shaped soul that what they witnessed was wrong but still allowed my friend to be sacrificed like a lamb on the altar of disdain. That altar still drips, and it's time we, as a faith community, take the lead in destroying it.

The apostle James, brother of Jesus, wrote that faith without works is dead. Faith without a demonstration that you're a better person for that faith isn't real. A faith that doesn't aim to redeem what's lost is counterfeit. *Faith doesn't demand perfection or even success in doing good. But it does require intent and effort.*

In Christianity, this faith is demonstrated in many ways, one profound example being a quest for fairness, or "justice in action." There is a new opportunity for people of faith to do their part in upholding and enforcing civil rights for all school-aged children.

Civil rights are rights that all citizens of a society should have, such as the right to receive fair treatment from the law. Most people contend that a person should have the right not to be abused, yet we've not been adamant enough that our children receive this right in school. We may *say* they should, but we've not mustered the cultural pressure or moral courage to enforce it.

Though Focus on the Family has bravely denounced bullying, there has yet to be a formal program, complete with curriculum, that helps churches and parachurch organizations combat school-based bullying from a Christian perspective. Until now.

# THE PROTECTORS

The Protectors (theprotectors.org) is a faith-based answer to bullying on school campuses. It provides teachers, ministers, and leaders the curriculum they need to minister to bullies, victims, the parents of both bullies and victims, and bystanders. It provides insight to become redemptive forces for good and to forge courage and self-regard.

It's clear in light of mounting school violence, with revenge against bullying as a primary motive, that teachers, administrators, and staff cannot tackle bullying alone. Our communities need faith-based organizations to fulfill their moral obligation to combat this cruel injustice and its catastrophic fallout.

## HELP FOR BYSTANDERS

This is a key group to The Protectors program because bullies love audiences that won't intervene—in fact they bank on it. It's our moral obligation to help others when it's within our power to act (e.g., Proverbs 3:27). Unfortunately, most bystanders have never received training to confidently and safely address bullying.

Bullying provides an excellent opportunity for peers to exercise courage. Currently, destructive peer pressure stops many kids from speaking out. The Protectors facilitates another form of peer pressure: one that encourages respect for all students, affirming their God-given dignity.

## HELP FOR VICTIMS

The Protectors helps victims realize that they aren't alone and that it's not their fault. Our curriculum helps students take the action necessary to protect themselves in warding off shame, humiliation, and self-hatred.

## HELP FOR BULLIES

The Protectors encourages empathy and prayer for bullies. Again, most are created by coercive parenting. Most are not born any more aggressive than other kids (a common misconception). At the same time, they must be confronted, both for the benefit of others and for their own good. When possible, bullies should be connected with mentors who can help them move beyond their antisocial behavior.

## HELP FOR PARENTS

Few experiences are more crushing than watching your child being bullied and feeling helpless. The Protectors helps parents understand why bullies focus on select targets, shows them what they can do today to help protect their child, demonstrates how to avoid bullying in the future, and teaches how to nurture their child's wounded spirit.

The Protectors also provides parents of kids who bully with information to help their child become well-adjusted and more compassionate toward others.

# CORE PRINCIPLES

The Protectors teaches five core principles, found throughout the Bible, to help children protect themselves and others from the nefarious influences of bullying.

## 1. THE POWER OF CLARITY

It is not God's will that children are humiliated and shamed in school. It's important that we possess clarity about this, because clarity is essential to having the confidence necessary to confront bullying. Bullies *know* that people are reluctant to step forward and confront them, largely due to moral ambiguity. They count on this reluctance, taking our confusion and converting it to their advantage.

## IT IS NOT GOD'S WILL THAT CHILDREN ARE HUMILIATED AND SHAMED IN SCHOOL.

Clarity produces conviction, and conviction provides strength. Victims need strength and invigoration because bullies are especially good at making victims and bystanders believe that their sense of justice is wrong and that the bully's view of life is right. With clarity, we see the wicked deception of bullying that harms a child both psychologically and spiritually. Many victims tell researchers that they think they're losing their grip on reality. In this way, bullies are similar to terrorists and cultists with their use of propaganda, defined as "ideas or allegations spread deliberately to further one's cause or to damage an opposing cause."[3] Bullies don't just dominate and degrade. They propagate an untrue worldview, that others (of their choosing) aren't worthy of innate value and worth.

## 2. THE AFFIRMATION OF BASIC RIGHTS

Whether or not you've been told otherwise, you have basic rights. Remember, our knowledge of sin is set upon the fundamental understanding that people are separate beings. One person ends and another begins. God expects people to respect that separateness. Bullies do not. When we mistreat our separateness, we sin.

Dr. Kenneth Haugk and Ruth Koch created a list of basic human rights from the Bible. They write in *Speaking the Truth in Love: How to Be an Assertive Christian:*

We are created in God's image—so Genesis 1:27 tells us, and we believe it. We are loved by God—so John 3:16 tells us, and we believe it. There are no distinctions to be made among us—so Galatians 3:28 tells us, and we believe it. We are priests, all of us, a royal priesthood—so 1 Peter 2:9 tells us, and we believe it. These are the good earth from which our basic human rights spring.

Each person has the right to be treated respectfully.

Each person has the right to say no without explanation and without guilt.

Each person has the right to slow down and take time to think.

Each person has the right to change his or her mind.

Each person has the right to ask for what he or she wants.

Each person has the right to ask for information.

Each person has the right to make mistakes.

Each person has the right to make choices and accept the consequences of those choices.

Each person has the right to own and express his or her own feelings.

Each person has the right to ask for help.

Each person has the right to maintain a separate self that is accountable to God and independent of the expectations, the approval, or the influences of others.[4]

The Protectors teaches these truths and adds the following:

All people have the right to withhold their good gifts from others if they discover that their good gifts (such as kindness) are not only destroyed but also used against them. This wise approach toward relationships should never be mistaken for a want of revenge.

Bullying expert Sam Horn, who has helped many learn how to better handle the bullies in their lives, created the following list of personal Clarity Rules that The Protectors believes schoolchildren should be taught as well:

(1) I have clarity that my definition of a healthy relationship is one in which I have the freedom to think and act for myself.

(2) I have clarity that I choose to believe the best of people, and I give them the benefit of the doubt until they prove me wrong.

(3) I have clarity that it is my responsibility to speak up if someone crosses the line of common decency.

(4) I have clarity that I will speak up if someone tries to intimidate me.

(5) I have clarity that I will walk tall so bullies won't perceive I'm weak.

(6) I have clarity that I will ask myself, "What's my culpability?" so that I do not unwittingly contribute to or perpetuate a bully's mistreatment of me.

(7) I have clarity that I will set and state limits in advance so people know my boundaries and ethical thresholds.

(8) I have clarity that I want to serve as a role model for my loved ones that we do not passively endure someone verbally abusing us.

(9) I have clarity that I will not volunteer to be a victim, and I will remove myself from a relationship in which someone is trying to control or own me.

(10) I have clarity that life is a blessing, not a burden, and I will not allow bullies to undermine my sanity or that of my loved ones.

(11) I have clarity that I am responsible for my physical and mental health, and I take appropriate action to improve unsafe situations.

(12) I have clarity that I do not give myself up and I do not give up on myself.[5]

## 3. CLARITY THROUGH BODY LANGUAGE

Keep in mind that bullies assess our clarity in a situation. They do this initially by reading our body language, which behaves like a traffic light: Don't Go There. Proceed With Caution. Proceed and Walk All Over Me. The Protectors teaches that victims invite or repel abuse by how they hold themselves.

For instance, have you noticed how bullies approach their victims when they are seated, and, remarkably, the victims remain seated? We teach children never to sit when being bullied. They should stand, put their hands on their hips, making sure to pull their shoulders back and look the person in the eyes.

Such training is also helpful in warding off adult predators. Bullies and related criminals look for people who exhibit what they call a "victim's stance":

► Faces pointed down

► Eyes too quick to make eye contact with others; eyes unfocused

► Hunched shoulders

► Arms that are close to their bodies, revealing a more protective pose

► Short, unsure steps

The Protectors teaches kids how to tower, not cower. For example:

► Stand up straight

► Chest out instead of in

► Steady eye contact with level chin

► Walk with purpose and energy

- ► Look confident while seated
- ► Girls: Don't carry your books by hugging them to your chest, which makes your shoulders curl forward.

## 4. THE POWER OF COMMAND

Many instances of bullying have been safely halted with words of conviction spoken with boldness, even when the person felt scared while saying them. Mark Galli, managing editor of *Christianity Today* and author of *Jesus Mean and Wild: The Unexpected Love of an Untamable God,* told me how he stopped someone much larger than him from beating up a kid who was unable to defend himself.

Galli said forcefully, "Stop it!"

"What are you going to do, Galli?" said the bully, knowing Galli was smaller than him.

"I'm not going to fight you. I just want you to stop it."

His words acted like a force field around his friend. The mere naming and acknowledgment of bullying was enough to stop the bully, who left.

My own experience bears this out as well. While in the locker room at Glencoe High School, in Hillsboro, Oregon, where I grew up, I saw a classmate pick on a mentally challenged student. He was shoving him and harassing him with shaming words, and almost every guy in the room bristled. It made me sick inside. Others told me later they felt the same way.

His prey tried to avoid him, but there's only so far you can go when you're wet and have a towel around your waist. It wasn't like he could go out in the hall to escape. I'm sure the bully knew that.

The sounds this kid made haunt me to this day. He grunted low, rumbling worry. His deep-throated protests, a mixture of fear and anger, shook his chest and curled up in a tone that said, *Stop!*

*You're hurting me!* He was being tormented, and since he knew only a few words, they failed him.

He was in over his head. He was the kind of kid who needed the goodwill others afforded him almost every day. And when he didn't get it, he was like a stranger in a foreign land. He needed people to be decent or at least neutral. He was no match for man's lower nature.

I've never been a big person. I'm like my Irish father, smaller and sinewy. The bully outweighed me and knew how to wrestle. Though I was a scrappy athlete, I knew I'd have my hands full if I confronted him, that he could likely throw me around. My life would have been easier if I'd kept my mouth shut like everyone else.

But indignation (which in Greek means to have "much to grieve") burned within me. I couldn't stand what I was seeing, and I didn't want to live with the corrosive feeling of cowardice—knowing the right thing to do but failing to do it because of fear.

I spoke up. Here's all I said: "Jimmy, knock it off!"

I made no appeals to morality. No shaming words. We knew he was a jerk, so why be predictable? Just a simple command spoken with both fear and bravery.

He stopped immediately, though he said something dumb, designed to save face.

I couldn't stop the words from coming out of my mouth. It's as if they had their own will, their own power source, an appointment with fate. I was scared and I was relieved, like a bubble of anxiety had been burst and I was free to breathe again. His domination of that kid was dominating me and the other guys as well. He had control over us, too, until one person spoke up.

I'm proud of what I did for a boy whose name I can't remember. For a person with whom I don't think I ever had a true conversation, other than with our eyes.

Numerous others have the same story to tell. One person

# PASSAGES FOR THE PROTECTORS

You shall love the Lord your God with all your heart, with all your soul, with all your strength, and with all your mind, and your neighbor as yourself. (Luke 10:27 NKJV)

The Lord has told you, human, what is good;
He has told you what he wants from you:
To do what is right to other people,
Love being kind to others,
And live humbly, obeying your God.
(Micah 6:8 NCV)

Do to others what you want them to do to you. (Matthew 7:12 NCV)

The Lord is righteous, he loves justice; upright men will see his face. (Psalm 11:7)

I, the Lord, love justice; I hate robbery and wrongdoing. (Isaiah 61:8 NEB)

Hate evil, love good; maintain justice. (Amos 5:15)

We urge you, brothers, warn those who are idle, encourage the timid, help the weak. (1 Thessalonians 5:14)

Be strong and courageous. The Lord himself goes before you and will be with you; he will never leave you nor forsake you. Do not be afraid; do not be discouraged. (Deuteronomy 31:7–8)

> In love a throne will be established; in faithfulness a man will sit on it—one from the house of David—one who in judging seeks justice and speeds the cause of righteousness. (Isaiah 16:5)
>
> Have I not commanded you? Be strong and courageous. Do not be terrified; do not be discouraged, for the Lord your God will be with you wherever you go. (Joshua 1:9)
>
> David also said to Solomon his son, "Be strong and courageous, and do the work. Do not be afraid or discouraged, for the Lord God, my God, is with you. He will not fail you or forsake you until all the work for the service of the temple of the Lord is finished" (1 Chronicles 28:20).

acting with even partial bravery not only promotes justice and goodness, he also grows moral courage, which can't be learned from a book. It must be created by the exercise of one's will in the quest to further the common good.

## 5. THE POWER OF TWO

One person who stands up for a victim has a good chance of defusing the situation with nothing more than a few spoken words. The Protectors helps those who guide youth to teach that success against bullies and toward being good increases dramatically when two (or more) people behave this way. The power of two is not only beneficial to others when it comes to moral courage, it's good to those people personally.

We call this the Power of Two, and it's found throughout the Bible. In the Old Testament we see Joshua and Caleb, after tearing their clothing in both grief and anger, stand against an entire community who did not want to enter the Promised Land and said they would have rather died in Egypt or in the desert (Numbers 14).

Jesus often sent His disciples out in pairs to complete tasks that one person could do but that were better done with two (Matthew 21:1; Mark 14:13). John the Baptist sent two disciples to ask Jesus a question when one would have sufficed (Luke 7:18). The disciples sent two men to get Peter when one would have worked (Acts 9:38). And Ecclesiastes says that though one may be overpowered, two can defend themselves better (4:12).

It's clear: *Two people in accord make a much stronger impression than one.*

# WHY WE RECOGNIZE INDIGNITIES

Jill Carattini, senior associate writer at Ravi Zacharias International Ministries, explains why indignities cut deeply and tells how they should move us to oppose them:

> Christians, Civil Rights activists, and grandparents take us aside and emphatically declare, "This is not the way it's supposed to be!" Comparable, yet all the more disturbed, were the cries of the Hebrew prophets of Scripture. Writes Isaiah, "The envoys of peace weep bitterly. The highways lie waste. . . . Covenants are broken; witnesses are despised; there is no regard for man" (Isaiah 33:7–8). Why do we want to scream "injustice!" when we stare into its cold eyes? Why do we look at darkness . . . and declare: "This is not the way it's supposed to be!" Perhaps we know inherently something we do not always recognize practically: We were created for far more.
>
> The prophets saw glaringly what we sense faintly. To us injustice is injurious to our sense of dignity. But to the prophets injustice is a catastrophic attack on the very character of God and the intrinsic dignity that God has given us. The spirit of man, said Matthew Henry, is the candle of God. Let us ever be sensitive to winds that try to extinguish life, and with burning hearts remember the significance of life that is made in the image of God.[6]

# DR. JAMES DOBSON ON VICTIMIZATION

By defending the least popular child in the classroom, the teacher is demonstrating that she respects everyone and that she will fight for anyone who is being treated unfairly.

Children love justice, and they're very uneasy in a world of injustice and abuse. Therefore, when we teach children kindness and respect for others by insisting on civility in our classrooms and in our homes, we're laying a foundation for human kindness in the world of adulthood to come. . . . While you are working behind the scenes to protect your child from abuse, you must not make him feel victimized beyond the immediate circumstance. It is very easy to give a boy the idea that the world is out to get him. That overarching sense of victimization is terribly destructive. It paralyzes a person and makes him throw up his hands in despair.

Once he yields to the insidious notion that he can't win, that he is set up for failure, he becomes demoralized. The will to overcome adversity is weakened.

The human personality grows through mild adversity, provided it is not crushed in the process. . . . In far too many homes, bullied kids are agitated, frustrated, and desperate for a way out, which may begin to explain the popularity of *Spider-Man,* a $400-million box-office smash. The movie is essentially a fantasy about a bullied teen who develops superpowers, transcends his circumstances, and dedicates himself to protecting others. It has struck a chord with audiences worldwide, young and old, who can, unfortunately, relate to the character's plight. [7]

# CHANGE WON'T COME UNTIL WE GET INVOLVED

Frank Peretti, novelist and wounded healer, has taken an uncompromising stance against bullying in two powerful books: *No More Bullies* and *No More Victims*. He notes that our society, and especially the Christian community, has been slow to discuss sensitive subjects, and that it needs clarity regarding whether bullying is right or wrong.

> We must ask ourselves, is it wrong? Consider your answer carefully. If the answer is yes, that immediately raises another question: Then why do we allow it? Why do parents, teachers, teacher's assistants, fellow students, friends at school and church, coworkers, extended family members, and others see it happening, hear it happening, and know it's happening but fail to take it seriously? If devaluing human life—and thereby mocking God's creation—is wrong, why do so many do so little to stop it? Worse yet, why do so many participate as part of the problem? . . .
>
> The message a bully sends is a mockery of God's handiwork, a lie that slanders God's nature and negates His love for us.[8]

Peretti was born with cystic hygroma, a birth defect that causes bodily fluids to back up around the head and neck, causing infection and other unpredictable occurrences.

> My tongue began to swell, and before long, it was hanging out of my mouth, oozing a fluid that turned to a black scab when it dried. I drooled constantly, leaving bloody, blackish residue around my mouth and chin, down the front of my clothes, and on my pillow.[9]

As a boy, he viewed himself as ugly, monstrous. In turn, monsters became his friends and "associates."

> [Monsters were] ugly, misunderstood, abused—creatures

who escaped from their cages, traps, and laboratories, scared everyone, broke things, and got back at the unfeeling people who abused them. They may have been victims, but they turned around and made victims of others.[10]

The sensitive boy had more troubles than most could imagine. He needed a special measure of grace from those around him. Instead he received tremendous humiliation. The torment from classmates continued.

He, like other bullied children, wanted to escape school, but authority had its standards. "You have to be there. You have no choice. You have to go. You have to be in that situation. You can't change anything."[11] He felt fate was against him.

Those to whom you look for love, shelter, and protection tell you to ignore your tormentors, stay away from them. Ignore them? Let's be honest: Ignoring is acting, and nothing more—acting as though the words or actions of your oppressors don't hurt.[12]

If you've spent any time on a Christian campus, you'll discover that such places are not immune to student-on-student abuse.

Let's talk about all those squeaky-clean students attending conservative colleges. They know their Bibles. They worship and pray at all the chapel services. They're out to spread the good news and change their world for the glory of God. And yet, when you get a chance to observe the social fabric on campus, it's sad to discover that things haven't changed much since junior and senior high school. The upperclassmen find it easy to put the underclassmen in their place. The jocks laugh and needle the non-athletes; the girls establish their social cliques and close the door to outsiders. Derogatory names and rumors float around freely. The very mention of certain names produces snickers among the elite in the student lounge.[13]

Peretti cannot forget his days of being bullied with no protector. He doesn't want the rest of us to forget either:

At the time of this writing, I'm close to fifty years of age, but I still remember the names and can see the faces of those individuals who made my life a living nightmare, day after day after day, during my childhood. I remember their words, their taunts, their blows, their spittle, and their humiliations. As I review my life, I think of all the decisions I shied away from, all the risks I dared not take, all the questions I never asked, all the relationships I didn't pursue, simply because I didn't want to be hurt again.[14]

I'm convinced that cruelty in and of itself is not fruitful, and to the fullest extent of my power, I won't allow it. I'm not impressed by the old argument that cruelty toughens us up for life. That's tantamount to saying it's right. Life is cruel enough by itself, thank you, with endless opportunities to suffer. Given that, one kind word or one encouraging touch teaches more lessons than one hundred cruelties. . . .

Maybe we're entering a new era in which bullying and the intimidation of other people are at last consigned to their rightful place alongside racism, hate-mongering, drunk driving, littering, spitting in public, and passing gas at parties. . . . People are slowly waking up to the prolonged impact of the problem—that bullies in school often grow up to be bullies in the home, abusing their spouses and children and perpetuating the downward spiral.[15]

After Columbine, a popular Christian musician wrote a song commemorating the life and death of a young woman who at the time was believed to have been murdered because of her faith. What we need to hear from the Christian community are songs that encourage Christians to proactively oppose bullying. Songs that make an appeal to common human dignity, that awaken moral courage on behalf of everyone, especially the weak, the persecuted, and the isolated.

A culture defines itself by what it rejects. Or, as G. K. Chesterton wisely observed, "Art, like morality, consists of drawing the line somewhere." Liberal or conservative, Christian or not, most of us agree: We need to say no to bullying because it is against our best interests.

In addition to the wicked boss I described earlier, I had a coworker who bullied as well. I'm still amazed, years later, at how one person can be allowed to keep an entire department or business on edge, worrying about when her petty wrath will strike.

This woman yelled at people she didn't like. She spread rumors behind their back, yet smiled to their face. She was eventually confronted, which was far too little and too late for many. I then heard her tell a colleague she'd enlisted in her campaigns of slander and libel to stop talking because "We can't do that anymore." This adult woman said it like a schoolgirl who'd had her hand slapped by the principal.

She didn't reduce or eliminate her campaigns against others because she felt inside the marrow of her being a universal love for the brotherhood of man. Rather, she'd been threatened with consequences if she continued her wicked ways. That's the language of the jungle, the native tongue of bullies. We must become fluent in it, or victims all around us will continue to suffer.

I have never seen a bully come to his or her senses the way others whom they hurt want them to or hope they will. People usually change either by inspiration or desperation, and sometimes the two are linked. Each bully in my life only changed through desperation, and only when a just and fair person demanded accountability—only when justice through the redemptive medium of courage *forced* them to change.

Please take a moment and think about bullying you've undergone. Did the bully change because he or she suddenly gained empathy and compassion for others? If you're in the vast majority, the answer is a resounding no. So why do we expect our kids, our most prized possession, to hold out for the exception? Their waiting in vain will bring them down and others down with them.

The Protectors wants kids to get a better education, to learn how to handle conflict redemptively, to make their school a safer place, to know how to avoid abuse, to sidestep or overcome anxiety and depression, and to develop moral courage early in life, greatly increasing their chances of adulthood success. If some or all of these stir passion in you, please join or support The Protectors, and share the opportunities with your pastors, your Sunday school teachers, your Awana teachers, your Scout leaders . . . anyone who can make a difference.

# WHERE, PARENTS, SHALL COURAGE BE FOUND?

We want character but without unyielding conviction; we want strong morality but without the emotional burden of guilt or shame; we want virtue but without particular moral justifications that invariably offend; we want good without having to name evil; we want decency without the authority to insist upon it; we want moral community without any limitations to personal freedom. In short, we want what we cannot possibly have on the terms that we want it.

—James David Hunter[1]

Be men of courage; be strong.

—1 Corinthians 16:13

Before departing on a cruise up and down the Pacific Coast with my family, I heard through the pounding public-address system an announcement that, in case of emergency, men should exercise selfless courage and allow women and children to enter the lifeboats first. I laughed, not at the call for masculine courage (a significant dynamic of *thumos*), but at the wishful thinking of the cruise line and, by extension, our culture. The only reason such a strange throwback to a bygone era (of male chivalry) is able to survive today is that such an (unfortunately) outdated perspective has yet to be challenged in the courts.

Many men now aren't even inclined to exercise the courtesy of giving a seat to a woman or child on a train or bus en route to a safe destination, let alone a vessel about to sink to the bottom of the deep blue sea. If they survived the disaster after being forced to wait for lifeboats, they'd likely hit the cruise line and the crew with unprecedented litigation. And our gender-scrubbing society would applaud the class-action lawsuits.

In March 1954, my parents came to the States along the same route as the *Titanic* (*sans* fateful icebergs). The swells were still troublesome, so much so that Poseidon extended their voyage two days and shifted the cargo so much that the off-keel boat struggled to make progress. My mother was seasick from the start and didn't feel better till she spotted America's eastern shore, nine days later. I sometimes think of them retracing that course, my mother below, sipping soda and trying to swallow a saltine cracker, and my hardy father, drinking Guinness near the bow, incapable of sea sickness. Had calamity arisen, I know what decision he would have made.

One memorial in Washington, D.C., is a waterfront statue honoring the men who died on and around the *Titanic*. Seventy-four percent of the women passengers survived that 1912 catastrophe; 80 percent of the men perished after relinquishing seating that with even a moderate display of physical strength could have been theirs.

The eighteen-foot granite *Titanic* monument displays a man with arms outstretched, signifying both sacrifice and affection. It was erected in 1931 by "the women of America" to show their gratitude. The inscription reads:

> To the brave men who perished in the wreck of the Titanic. . . .
> They gave their lives that women and children might be saved.

Such courage does not inspire us as it should. That act of corporate bravery played such a miniscule role in the 1997 blockbuster film as to constitute a kind of flag-burning insult. (Women can be and are courageous too; my point here isn't that courage relates to one gender or the other but rather that we no longer clearly understand, cultivate, and practice courage on the whole.) Writes Christina Hoff Sommers, critic of radical feminism and defender of America's young boys:

> [Today, such] male gallantry makes many women nervous, suggesting (as it does) that women require special protection. It implies the sexes are objectively different. It tells us that some things are best left to men. Gallantry is a virtue that dare not speak its name.[2]

Job lamented, "Where shall wisdom be found?" (Job 28:12 KJV). Today we add to his timeless cry the demise of courage, because without it our children will still have life but not really live. As you'll see, reading to them tales of

**KIDS NEED TO SEE AT LEAST ONE PARENT LIVING COURAGE, WHICH IS FAR MORE CAUGHT THAN TAUGHT.**

courage, important as that is, will not get the job done. Kids need to see at least one parent living courage, which is far more caught than taught.

# COURAGE AND CULTURE

We're involved in our community: Church. Coaching. PTA. Fellowship. Speaking engagements. In that cultural loop, I don't hear courage talked about much at all. When we do talk about courage, it's almost always ascribed to physical feats that demand bravery and some level of mastery over fear. Or to someone's weight loss, which usually has more to do with ambition and desire.

The word *courage* was once reserved for the kind of behavior requiring sacrifice and suffering on behalf of a person for the common good, part of the definition of righteousness that's found especially in the Bible. We've discarded this meaning for a more inclusive, less demanding, and more me-centered understanding, and we as a nation are damaged by this reduction.

Moral courage is a cornerstone virtue upon which other virtues gain their strength and stability. Most philosophers, sages, and spiritual leaders tell us that without courage, our kids won't really create hope, faith, and love and their residual blessings because all of those demand risk of some kind. Courage helps us get through risk and face its associated fears in order to reap the benefits of virtuous living. Courage gives us power to be better spouses, parents, employers, employees, friends, citizens of earth and heaven. Courageous people do better in life; we need to show our children what it is, what it's not, and how to obtain it.

When I speak at conferences and workshops, I often ask people to think of examples of moral courage. The most common answers are the rescue attempts during the 9/11 terrorist attacks and what our fighting men and women are doing in Iraq and Afghanistan. Those are good answers. But when I point out that our armed-forces combat troops comprise less than one percent of our population, an awkward silence follows. A nation can't live vicariously through less than one of every hundred citizens.

# COURAGE AND CHURCH

I wrote earlier about my experience regarding church messages and Sunday school curricula. In the former, courage rarely surfaces at all (except in terms of either sharing God's salvation message with others or giving more money to the church than we think we can afford). In the latter, it's almost exclusively a defensive kind of courage—courage to say no when someone wants a kid to do something bad. I call this boundary courage, which is both valuable and necessary. However, what about offensive courage, the courage required to confront injustice, to help the timid and the weak, and to bolster the well-being of a community?

Search for "courage" on the Web sites of America's most popular preachers, and you'll be sadly disappointed. During a pulpit age where relationships take center stage, courage should be an intrinsically foundational subject, since no relationship grows meaningfully without the conviction and love that courage provides.

It also takes courage to exercise many spiritual gifts (1 Corinthians 12; Ephesians 4; Romans 12). Ephesians tells us these gifts, which help us become apostles, prophets, evangelists, and pastors/teachers, have the ability to grow us into "mature manhood" and to stop us from being thrown around by damaging doctrines. Not only this, they also have the ability to help us combat human cunning, craftiness, and deceit. In so doing, we are better able to speak the truth in love.

Romans tells us that the gifts given to us by God's Holy Spirit include wise speech and the ability to put the deepest knowledge into words. Use wise language and you'll find that you'll inevitably be standing against something—usually a popular cultural appetite. Speaking this way requires courage. What would be immensely helpful to the average churchgoer is learning that though these are good gifts from God, the exercise of them often requires an accompanying decision to exercise courage.

When I got married in my mid-twenties, I had no idea how much courage was required to really love someone, as opposed to doing what's needed to give the appearance that we were getting along. Compromise is essential to marital happiness, but so is exercising the courage necessary to confront what must be confronted and doing it without either yelling or whimpering. *Our lives expand or contract in proportion to our courage.* Our divorce rates aren't going to decrease without an increasing influx of courage.

When Dr. James Dobson was an elementary teacher, he couldn't understand why so many adults were cowards. He writes regarding kids who were picked on by bullies, "I find it difficult to comprehend why adults have to be encouraged to shield a vulnerable child whose defenses have crumbled."[3] His frustration cannot be fully grasped unless seen in light of Mahatma Gandhi's intimate comprehension of the dynamics of domination and resistance: "Bullies are always to be found where there are cowards."[4]

## COURAGE REQUIRES THAT WE STAND *AGAINST* SOMETHING AND SOMEONE.

I think one of the main reasons we have failed to exercise courage on behalf of the weak and the needy is that doing so requires more than standing for something and someone. Courage requires that we stand *against* something and someone. Standing against a bully means we name his behavior as wrong and dangerous. The spirit of our age has intimidated and silenced us. We've had our indignation toward wickedness drained by political and "theological" correctness.

For many Christian parents, teachers, and coaches, our training tells us to pray about a troubling situation and then get out of the way. Additional action is often deemed unnecessary, even unspiritual. God, we've been told, has everything under control—no need for us to get our hands dirty in life's ugliness.

WHERE, PARENTS, SHALL COURAGE BE FOUND?

Too many of us have our spiritual hands in our spiritual pockets jingling coins instead of spending them. Our courage has atrophied, and we're not the sources of salt and light we're meant to be. Wrote Theodore Roosevelt, "You have to have courage. I don't care how good a man is, if he is timid, his value is limited. The timid will not amount to much in this world. I want to see a good man able to hold his own in active life against the force of evil."[5] So do many others. But how?

# *MY* COURAGE MATTERS

In the months after 9/11, Senator John McCain, Vietnam veteran and perhaps America's most well-known prisoner of war, was asked to explain to the nation why courage matters as part of America's response to our worst domestic terrorist attack on American soil.

Courage is a subject few know more intimately than McCain (at least among those who have lived to tell their story). In 1967, McCain's A–4 Skyhawk was shot down by an antiaircraft missile, landing in Truc Bach Lake. He'd broken both arms and a leg after ejecting, and after he regained consciousness, a mob gathered around him and tore his clothing off. He was tortured by Vietnamese soldiers, who bayoneted his left foot and groin and crushed his shoulder with a rifle butt. He was transported to the Hoa Lo Prison, also known as the Hanoi Hilton.

McCain was placed in a cell and interrogated daily. When he refused to provide any information to his captors, he was beaten until he lost consciousness. When the North Vietnamese discovered his father was commander of all U.S. forces in Vietnam, McCain was offered a chance to return home. Seeing it as a public relations stunt by his captors, he refused.

McCain signed an anti-American propaganda message (something he most regrets of his time as a POW), written in Vietnamese, as a result of rigorous and brutal torture that rendered him incapable of raising his arms above his head. When the Vietnamese decided they couldn't use the statement, they tried to force him to sign a second, and this time he refused. He received two to three beatings per week because of his ongoing refusal.

He was held as a POW for five-and-a-half years, almost five years longer than if he'd accepted the earlier offer of release. During his military career, he received a Silver Star, a Bronze Star, the Legion of Merit, the Purple Heart, and a Distinguished Flying Cross.

Compare McCain's courage with that of the pampered celebrity who talks about her "courageous battle" with losing twenty pounds (when I heard one talk about the "courage" required to get breast implants, I had to go for a walk), and you see just how far our understanding of courage has slipped. McCain explains:

> We have attributed courage to all manner of actions that may indeed be admirable but hardly compare to the conscious self-sacrifice on behalf of something greater than self-interest that once defined courage. We have come to identify one or more of the elements of courage—fortitude, discipline, daring, or righteousness, for example—as the entire virtue.[6]

Courage, writes McCain, is

> that rare moment of unity between conscience, fear, and action, when something deep within us strikes the flint of love, of honor, of duty. . . . It is an acute awareness of danger, the sensation of fear it produces, and the will to act in spite of it. I think it is the highest quality of life attainable by human beings. . . . I think God meant us to be courageous so that we could know better how to live, how to love what, and as, He commands us to love.[7]

> It is not enough to be honest and just and demand that we be treated honestly and justly by others. We must learn to

love honesty and justice for themselves, not just for their effect on our personal circumstances, but for their effect on the world, on the whole of human experience.[8]

McCain says there is one state of mind "that must always be present for courage to exist: fear. You must be afraid to have courage."[9] But one of our largest misunderstandings about courage is that it's synonymous with suffering. Suffering "is not by itself, courage; fearing what we choose to suffer, is."[10] Enduring an inescapable fate stoically is admirable, but it's not the same as courage. "Suffering stoically a terrible fate that you could have escaped, but that your convictions, your sense of honor, compelled you to accept, is."[11] In this way, courage enters the moral realm and is more than mental toughness or "grace under pressure," as Hemingway's peculiar phrase defined it. The 50th Anniversary edition of John F. Kennedy's *Profiles in Courage* records the definition of courage by Profile-in-Courage-Award-recipient Congressman John Lewis (D-GA) for his civil rights leadership:

> Courage is a reflection of the heart. It is a reflection of something deep within the man or woman or even a child who must resist and must defy an authority that is morally wrong. Courage makes us march on despite fear and doubt on the road toward justice. . . . Courage is not rooted in reason but rather courage comes from a divine purpose to make things right.
>
> When you stand up to injustice, when you refuse to let brute force crush you, when you love the man who spits on you or calls you names or puts a lighted cigarette in your hair, you come to believe that righteousness will always prevail. Just hold on.[12]

What's more, anyone can do it! "I've known any number of physically fit cowards. I've known any number of self-assured cowards. And I've known quite a few humble, physically delicate people who had a lion's courage when they needed it."[13]

Just as there are different degrees or manifestations of love, McCain explains that courage has variant forms as well. "The defensive kind of courage, the capacity to suffer with dignity, without losing hope, is a virtue that can be possessed by the physically strong and weak alike. . . . It must be voluntary, however, to be courage."[14]

We parents must grasp this vital distinction. Forcing a kid to do the right thing is not the same as building courage in her, which in turn builds other qualities (like respect). In order for behavior to cultivate the young soil of courage in our children, it must be voluntary, not coercive. They must first want to do the right thing, then receive encouragement to stay upon this gallant course, which means helping them handle fear.

> Face the experience with quiet assurance or with a look that reflects stark terror, screaming in anguish all the while. It doesn't really matter. What matters is that you faced it, lived it, and did so because your conscience compelled you to act. That is what gives courage its grandeur. Even Christ on the cross, my faith's most exalted example of courage, cried out in desperation, "Father, Father, why have You forsaken me?" Is it not Christ's reticence in a moment of agony that we worship? It is because he accepted his duty to love, a love incarnate—God become man to redeem humanity by love—and the awful suffering his duty demanded that we exalt the singular courage of his sacrifice.[15]

If someone doesn't love, then she will not be very courageous. Love motivates courage as bold service to others. Dr. Martin Luther King Jr. said:

> You don't have to have a college degree to serve. You don't have to make your subject and your verb agree to serve. You don't have to know about Plato and Aristotle to serve. You don't have to know Einstein's theory of relativity to

serve. You only need a heart full of grace. A soul generated by love.[16]

McCain, like many younger men, thought courage would be there and be sustained when he needed it—all he had to do was call it forth. While imprisoned in Vietnam, though, "I would use my anger to prime the pump of my courage and provoke confrontations with the enemy. But many times, when I was weary and somewhat forlorn, I just couldn't recover the strength to put myself in need of it." What bolstered his courage then, and what can bolster ours and our children's now? Being among others who feed courage. "Many times when I was brought back to my cell after an extended and physically challenging interrogation, the first thing I would do is tap on the wall to my neighbor."[17] The responses lifted his spirits. We and our children need brothers and sisters in courage, too.

Again, our children learn far more about courage from our behavior than our words. Living with cowardice is taxing enough on a person's soul. We parents should consider the additional sorrow of modeling such behavior, endeavoring instead to live out the fullness of virtue as we teach our children to weigh in their minds the consequences of not behaving courageously.

**OUR CHILDREN LEARN FAR MORE ABOUT COURAGE FROM OUR BEHAVIOR THAN OUR WORDS.**

# WHAT PARENTS SHOULD KNOW AND DO

Some argue that fear, not hatred or apathy, is the exact opposite of love. No matter the technicalities, we need to let our children know that while fear *is* a major enemy of love, it's always present when we're given the opportunity to grow courage or cowardice. Fear here is normal, and the fear isn't usually as apparent to others as we think. McCain's advice?

> Just move along quickly and things will likely turn out fine. . . . Don't let the sensation in your ear convince you that you're too weak to have courage. Fear is the opportunity for courage, not proof of cowardice. No one is born a coward. We were meant to love. And we were meant to have the courage for it. So be brave. The rest is easy.[18]

To give courage a chance to grow, we need to expose our children to the concept of honor, which is concerned with more than one's own dignity, important as that is. Honor is connected to other virtues, such as justice, loyalty, and fidelity. Honor values others and truth so much that it motivates a person to protect their value and worth. Honor, properly applied, says McCain, is "concerned with the rights of others."[19]

In order for kids to embrace honor, we need to help them cultivate dignity. This doesn't mean we encourage them to fight every force that threatens their dignity. It does mean they recognize that when their value is or has been under attack, sometimes wisdom dictates overlooking the offense, and sometimes wisdom signals responding in defense. This is a proactive self-worth, and living this way means our children are also more likely to both consider *and* defend the dignity and worth of others. My children know that when they have conflict with other kids, they need to ensure that they let their opponent retain his dignity. Not only does this often turn away an assailant's wrath, it likewise tends to keep children from making unnecessarily long-term foes.

With regard to their peer relationships and social status, to the factors of popularity and stability and being well-liked, the maverick senator says,

The child who rebukes a friend for cruelty to another might soon find the consequences were really not so terrible after all. On the contrary, other peers, not to mention the victimized child, might recognize the virtuousness of the act and be attracted to it and to its author. It should make it easier to take the risk of exercising virtue the next time. . . .

[We parents] have to believe that there really is no great significance to being popular. We have to believe that we love and are loved by our family, by our true friends, and from that love we become good.[20]

Additionally, we must help our children understand the distinction between outrage and anger, a distinction I've often missed. Anger might stimulate impetuous courage, but of all degrees of courage this is the least effective. *Outrage,* in this context, means to take moral offense at something. Outrage is tied closely to our understanding of *indignation,* which, as we have said, in the Greek is rendered to mean "much grief." To possess righteous indignation, our children need to see us grieve the pain and suffering of others. People's trials and troubles begin to take actual shape and form, then, for our kids, and this helps other people appear on their psychological radar screen as they build thoughtfulness, compassion, empathy, love, and courage in their hearts and minds.

This kind of growth takes practice, *and* it requires the freedom to make mistakes as they grow. Don't be too quick to point out that your son or daughter is getting too upset about something— listen to them, learn from them. If needed, do point out, lovingly, when your child is failing to express indignation over unrighteousness and injustice. We want our children to become *more* passionate, not less!

Now I want to introduce you to a man who, like John Mc-Cain, possessed such great moral fortitude that he believed he had no choice but to do the right thing, in part through the fastening on of his courage. We'll learn vital lessons—if we're brave enough not to flinch and look away.

CHAPTER

12

# TRAITS OF THE COURAGEOUS

To have courage for whatever comes in life—everything
lies in that.

—Mother Teresa

Courage helps us digest reality for breakfast and keep it down,
converting it into vital energy and momentum. It helps us overcome obstacles that might otherwise halt us. Courage is essential
to meaningful attainment and to our integrity, the definition of
which must expand if we want to help our children achieve the
real thing.

All good-willed parents want their kids to obtain healthy and
honorable achievement, but currently we're handcuffing them
with nice-sounding intentions that dissipate when applied to the
real world. Good behavior alone won't fly; it was never designed
to. We need to guide our children to achievement not fulfilled
upon the broken backs of others—which leaves in its wake resentment, bitterness, and cynicism—but instead toward achievement
that's nourishing for themselves and others. This is especially relevant in America, a nation awash in ambition, much of which is

good, some of which is bad. It takes courage to follow integrity because that often means taking the longer and harder route.

When a person possesses integrity, it means far more than whether or not she swore when she stubbed her toe on the leg of her desk. Explains Dr. Henry Cloud:

> When we talk about integrity, we are talking about being a whole person, an integrated person, with all of our different parts working well and delivering the functions that they were designed to deliver. It is about *wholeness* and *effectiveness* as people. It truly is "running on all cylinders."[1]

Our kids becoming *effective* people means that as children they begin to learn what it takes to be successful, *whole,* and integrated, as opposed to merely following traditions, fads, homilies, and platitudes. Otherwise they're in trouble—remember, too much sweetness and softness, too little wisdom and discernment turns children into victims, both now and later. Warns Cloud,

> You have known people who love, for example, without the benefit of judgment and reality testing. . . . *Strengths turn into weaknesses without the other parts of a person to balance them out.* In fact, historically, the word *diabolical* actually means "to compartmentalize." Things go "bad" when they are out of balance and integration. The person of "integrity" is a person of balanced integration of all that character affords.[2]

Buildings lack structural integrity when they're unable to carry their load in the way they were designed to provide shelter, and even inspiration. We lack integrity in the same way when our moral backbone, courage-unfortified, isn't strong enough to carry the weight of our own lives and when we lack sufficient power to donate our strength to others in need, providing protection and inspiration.

Helping our children obtain the courage necessary to produce moral integrity is so much more than turning them into what Thomas Merton called "little morality projects" defined exclusively by avoiding sin. We *should* avoid sin, in part, so that we move closer to God's bonfire blessing of an abundant and eternal life—this is the God-centered life He desires for everyone made in His image. But avoiding sin is just part of this God-glorifying journey; it's not the journey itself. Abundant living is the journey. A rich life is the peak toward which we want to guide our children, and our instruction should include the steps, skills, and virtues necessary to reach the top.

Once more, our lives lack integrity when they lack wholeness and balance. Our current definition of wholeness as personal piety is a major contributor to this sincere but precarious imbalance. Our children need wisdom and its corresponding virtues (e.g., shrewdness and ingenuity) in order to find this balance, and the courage it takes to graft wisdom into their lives.

Recall that *virtue,* a word closely associated with integrity, has as one of its meanings the word *force.* A virtuous person is defined by far more than what she *doesn't* do, what force she *doesn't* exert. She's also defined by what she does—her strength is hers to spend in proactivity or waste through inactivity. Fear of using force and its potential backlash is why nice spouses have repeated marriage woes, why nice bosses are eaten alive by sneaky employees, why nice coaches lead teams toward turmoil, and why nice kids get picked on at school. It takes courage to use force virtuously.

Please understand what I'm really saying. Being honest *is* intrinsic to integrity. It's foundational. But it's not the only quality our children need in order to possess integrity, and with it success. The main reason I'm making this distinction is that I'm around so many who've only been given this false script of personal piety. Some are oblivious to entire facets of reality; others ignore reality largely because they don't have the skills to face it well and fear the pain that might come their way if they did. They don't like conflict, and they haven't been trained to do it well, so their honesty-first policy goes out the window when they're unwilling to disagree truthfully with others when it's needed. Then their personal piety takes a hit anyway.

Somewhere inside they lie to themselves and stick to the just-be-nice-and-life-will-work-out-right approach. It's what they don't acknowledge and don't act upon that takes them out of the game of life. They miss or ignore important components of reality (top of the list: the inability to spot deceit in others and the boldness to confront it), and without the courage necessary to feel fear, really feel it, they don't push through toward a clearer view of life.

Much of our collective confusion would dissipate if it weren't for our fear about earning other people's disapproval, even when deep down we know (or could know) precisely the right thing to do. Courage helps us push past this fear with the force of virtue. *What are the traits that help grow the hardy fruit of courage?*

# A STORY FOR THE AGES

In *The Moses of Rovno: The Stirring Story of Fritz Graebe, a German Christian Who Risked His Life to Lead Hundreds of Jews to Safety During the Holocaust,* Presbyterian minister Douglas Huneke describes the behavior of a single soul whose tale of courage and bravery should be told to every child in every country. Songs should be written about the rare character of this unsung "Oskar Schindler"; his valorous life should be captured on film.

Holocaust survivor and renowned author Elie Wiesel said that "Graebe's courage justifies our faith in humankind." Rabbi Harold Schulweis said, "The world is hungry for moral heroes like Fritz Graebe. Because of him, they who knew the sadness of the disillusioned heart know also that there is an alternative to complicity with the enemies of humanity. They know that there is meaning to our belief that humanity was created in the image of God."[3]

But to some timid-hearted people, Graebe didn't behave like a Christian at all.

Herman Friedrich "Fritz" Graebe (1900–1986), a manager and engineer in charge of a German building firm in Ukraine, witnessed mass Nazi executions of Jews. Following the war he provided vital testimony in the Einsatzgruppen Trial (one of the subsequent Nuremberg Trials), invoking bitter persecution from many of his countrymen. He moved his family to San Francisco in 1948, where he lived until his death. He was honored as "righteous among the nations" by the Israelis.

Graebe was born in Gräfrath, a small town in the Rhineland, where the population was predominantly Roman Catholic. He was the eldest son of a poor Protestant couple: His father was a weaver, and his mother helped supplement the family income by working as a maid. After primary school, Herman went on to study at a technical college to become a licensed engineer. He completed his state-licensing examinations shortly after being married in 1924.

In 1931, Graebe joined the Nazi party. However, he broke with it in 1934, after boldly criticizing a Nazi campaign against Jewish businesses. Following this he was apprehended by the Gestapo and jailed for several months. He was subsequently released without trial.

From 1938 to 1941, Graebe participated as a civilian contractor in the construction of the "West Wall" fortifications on Germany's western border. In the summer of 1941, shortly after the Germans invaded the Soviet Union, Graebe was directed to report to the offices of the Reich Railway Administration in Lwow. His assignment was to recruit construction teams to help build and renovate structures essential for the maintenance of railroad communications in Ukraine. Arriving there in September, Graebe set up his head office and proceeded to deploy subsidiary offices throughout Soviet Ukraine. The Jewish work force employed by his company comprised some five thousand men and women.

As a large-scale civilian contractor with extensive connections, Graebe witnessed the atrocities perpetrated by the Germans and their Ukrainian henchmen against the helpless Jews. On October 5, 1942, he was present at a mass-killing site and saw how approximately five thousand Jewish men, women, and children were lined up in front of already dug pits, ordered to remove their clothing (some even folded it), and were cold-bloodedly executed by SS firing squads. Graebe would be haunted by what he saw until his death. After the war, his graphic accounts were incorporated into the evidence of the Nuremberg Trials.

In his efforts to rescue Jews from the Nazi destruction machine, Graebe could take advantage of his official position as the representative of the Josef Jung Company. By arguing that he was performing work essential for the German war effort, he acquired effective leverage over the German district commissioner and his subordinates. Graebe deliberately attracted and accepted more assignments and contracts than his company could possibly handle so as to employ more Jews. He would then go to great lengths to protect them and their families.

For example, in July 1942, Graebe learned that an imminent "liquidation action" was going to be directed against the Jews of Rovno, where he had 112 Jews working for him. Having obtained a "writ of protection" from the deputy district commissioner, he rushed with it to Rovno where, gun in hand, he managed to secure the release of 150 Jews. It was a very close call: Ukrainian policemen were already busy driving the ghetto inmates to their deportation train. Graebe marched the lucky ones away on foot, out of harm's clutches.

When, some months later, the Germans incarcerated the Jews of Zdolbunov in a ghetto and started deporting them, Graebe provided twenty-five workers with falsified "Aryan" identification papers. He subsequently transported them in stages, with his own car, to the far-flung company office in Poltava, hundreds of miles to the east. The Poltava branch was pure fiction: Graebe had set it up and maintained it at his own expense for the sole purpose of providing shelter for his Jewish workers. With the advance of the Red Army later in the war, the group was able to escape to the Russian side. Had the car been stopped at one of the numerous German roadblocks on the way, both rescuer and rescued would have been doomed.

In the course of time, Graebe's uneconomic policies and unconventional practices began to arouse the suspicion of his company chiefs. They wanted him recalled and put on trial for embezzlement. After the collapse of the German positions in eastern Poland, Graebe moved with his Jewish office team first to Warsaw and from there to the Rhineland. In September 1944, he defected with about twenty of his charges to the American lines, where he was still able to render valuable strategic advice concerning the West Wall.

From February 1945 until the autumn of 1946, Graebe worked closely with the War Crimes Branch of the U.S. Army on the preparation of the Nuremberg dossier on crimes committed by the Germans. He was the only German to testify for the prosecution. In 1948 he and his family emigrated to the United States.

Graebe's acts of righteousness, explains Huneke, "were not impulsive, solitary gestures, but involved, sustained commitment over a long period of time and entailed incredible risks."[4] He had to be away from his family constantly in order to carry out his redemptive work. He depleted his personal resources and suffered serious health consequences.

Like most rescuers, he disdained the label of hero. He referred to his acts as simple, often inadequate, tokens of human decency.

He told visitors, "I did what anyone could have done, should have done."[5]

## HOW IS COURAGE MADE?

One factor that made Graebe's life so remarkable is that by 1941, he was already forty-one years old, a husband and father, and a successful construction engineer. In other words, he had what we often call "The American Dream." He had worked hard to obtain material wealth and comfort. By most standards, he had a lot to lose. Huneke wondered why Graebe risked his life and the well-being of his family when most others wouldn't. His childhood reveals many clues.

Graebe grew up in a world of distinct right and wrong, but that sense of righteousness was always tempered by an equally strong sense of charity, a willingness to understand and appreciate the position of the other person.

He grew up with a brother, Erich, who was born with a crippling spinal deformity. Children ridiculed him, sometimes in front of their mother, Frau Graebe. They messed with the wrong mom. She scolded the boys for their thoughtlessness, then would soften her tone and ask the boys how they would feel if they were treated this way about a problem they couldn't fix. The teasing ended.

**HE SAW HIS MOTHER LIVE OUT EASY-TO-UNDERSTAND ACTS OF COURAGE.**

Frau often asked Fritz to envision himself in the shoes of those less fortunate, so much so that Graebe said it was normal for him to empathize with those less fortunate than him. That is, he developed the virtue of empathy as he saw his mother live out easy-to-understand acts of courage.

Graebe developed a debilitating stutter while in college, a problem he'd never before experienced. It embarrassed him so much that he stopped going to classes, but he eventually decided that things had to change. He bought a self-help book and practiced reading aloud in front of a mirror. He did this for almost four years.[6] His stuttering helped him feel empathy for others.

Graebe also admired courage in others.

The voting procedure in Gräfrath on November 12, 1933, was not like voting before. Though there were the usual curtained booths, no one was using them. Instead, the line of voters filed before a simple open desk. Standing behind the desk was a neighbor, Reinhard Bertram, who locals called "little Hitler" because he wielded a good deal of power. The voting setup was a clear message: People were free to vote in a booth, but such an action would be interpreted as opposition to the Party. Most everyone stayed in the line and awaited their opportunity to draw a highly coerced X on the paper in Bertram's sight.

But one man, Adolf Stocker, a highly respected and courageous community member, mustered the boldness to vote behind the curtain. "He strode to one of the booths, nodded to the awestruck crowd, took off his hat, entered the polling booth, ceremoniously closed the curtain, and cast his vote."[7]

The polling stations closed at 6:00 P.M. By 8:00 the results were in. Germany had "voted" for Hitler. In Gräfrath, there was only one "no" vote, and everyone knew who'd cast it. That night a line of torches snaked up the hillside to where Stocker and his family lived.

Fritz and Elizabeth Graebe lived nearby. They could see the crowd growing and the sky glowing brighter above the torchlights. Through a loudspeaker, someone shouted over and over, "What should we do with Stocker? What should we do with Stocker?" The crowd roared back in rhythmic response: "Aufhangen! Aufhangen! Hang him! Hang him!"[8]

Unexpectedly the mob stopped chanting and dispersed. It was believed that Stocker's two sons were forced to take part in this act of cowardly intimidation of a righteous man, that they were forced to climb the hill, torch in hand, and demand their father's execution. "Can you imagine that?" Graebe cried. "Those bastards! What a tragedy for Stocker. They made his sons do something terrible like that. Can you imagine that poor man in his house knowing that his sons were outside shouting such words?"[9]

I'm willing to bet that right now more readers have their eyes and minds glued to the "B" word than to (1) the atrocity against that Job-like man and (2) Graebe's powerful display of righteous indignation. We are so well-trained today to strain out this kind of gnat that, during my darker days, I worry we will never get it right. Our spiritual training is setting up today's Christians to behave like those people who marched up the hill—*one unfailing lesson about courage and righteousness is that when placed on the anvil, in desperation, few remain neutral. We are either for righteousness or against it.* Without tangible courage to draw from, we, like the churchgoing people of Germany, will be against it.

**WE HAVE BEEN TRAINED TO BE MORE CONCERNED WITH SOCIAL ETIQUETTE THAN WITH THE VIRTUE OF HATING SIN AND INJUSTICE.**

We have been trained to be more concerned with social etiquette than with the virtue of hating sin and injustice—than with creating justice as we are able. Part of following Jesus is the ability and willingness to call evil *evil*. But that's just the start: *We are to despise evil and act against it.* Hatred of evil is expressed neither through flowery language nor a perma-smile. Scholar Ben Witherington observes, "One could say that righteous anger is a prerequisite for ministry, for a person who has no capacity for righteous anger at the things that destroy humankind is a person who fails to be truly compassionate."[10]

Notice Witherington says "things that destroy humankind." This does not include the aggravation caused by getting cut off in traffic or having our cable television bill increase. *Righteous indignation is a response to events that dehumanize, not inconvenience.*

Selective standards are worthless when we ignore the Ultimate Standard (see Luke 10:27; John 13:34; 1 John 3:11–20; 4:7–12). These only lead to myopic living and nearly impenetrable self-righteousness. It's widely believed that Hitler found swearing, drinking, and premarital sex offensive. He viewed himself as highly ethical and principled, and he is one of history's most phenomenal gnat strainers. We're told plainly what Jesus thinks of that.

> Woe to you, teachers of the law and Pharisees, you hypocrites! You give a tenth of your spices—mint, dill and cummin. But you have neglected the more important matters of the law—justice, mercy and faithfulness. (Matthew 23:23)

Fritz Graebe hated evil. He was obstinate toward the arrogance and anti-Semitism of Nazi Party leaders. When he disputed them in public, he was dragged to a jail where he was given two books: The Bible, and Martin Luther's *Against the Robbing and Murdering Hordes of Peasants*, a polemic on the violence of the Peasants' Revolt in southwestern Germany in 1525. The Nazis used that writing to justify their atrocities against Jews, gypsies, and other groups deemed undesirable.

Graebe believed that in that conflict, Luther was on the wrong side and should have defended the peasants from the landlords. He shows us that the courageous are more concerned with justice than with tradition and popularity. They are willing to break with convention if that's where truth and justice lead.

They also stand up to authority, even religious authority. Though the true church was alive, the official church had deserted

Graebe, and was bent on destroying his moral foundation. We see this in a Lutheran pastor's visit to him in jail, his only pastoral visit.

"So you've offended the Fuehrer! Spoken out against him," the minister said firmly. "Herr Graebe, you should be ashamed of yourself. A man like you in jail—it is a disgrace to your family. The Third Reich needs you. It needs men of character with skills and commitment."[11]

Then he worked another angle upon Graebe, much like the devil in questioning Jesus in His extreme weakness after forty days in the wilderness. "Too much stubbornness can lead to trouble—perhaps even twenty or thirty years of it . . . you have an obligation to the Fatherland. . . . It is your Christian duty."[12]

Graebe was shrewd and astute enough to spot the argument's false pretense. But he couldn't sleep. He couldn't figure out how to avoid mandatory military service to a government exterminating an entire race. He also couldn't afford another confrontation with authorities, which would certainly land him back in prison (if not in a graveyard). So he staged an accident on his way to required registration for military duty. He purposely drove over two nail-studded boards, flattening all his tires.

Nearly an hour past the deadline, when police came by and asked why he hadn't seen the nail-studded boards, he lied and said he'd ambitiously left so early in the morning that he was too tired to see them. The police bought his false, full-of-fake-patriotism story and gave him a note that pardoned his tardiness. Graebe artfully manipulated his environment by staging a false event, feigning despair and frustrated nationalism that later allowed him to carry out his noble mission. As with every virtue, we need to point out to our children why and how such deception took place. It wasn't for selfish means. It was in service of a higher good. If Graebe had joined the military of the ruthless regime, he would not have been able to save those Jewish lives.

His subsequent lies were audacious and prevalent. He often worked himself up into outrageous performances before Nazi authority, pretending to possess far more power than he actually had. He falsified papers and provided small bribes—a cigar, a drink, a cigarette. One of his most useful fabrications was telling those who opposed him that he was under strict but secret orders from Berlin. He would milk this for all it was worth by saying, "Besides, it is better for you that you not know about Berlin."[13]

He yelled, "I have my deadlines, and if I do not make them, I will be court-martialed, not you—me! Do not disturb my labor column—I don't care if they are Jewish."[14] A lie upon a lie; he cared deeply that "they" were Jewish. They were why he risked his own life.

While on trial for a construction delay, Graebe worked himself into a carefully planned rage, turning the tables on the court and becoming their disrespectful judge.

> I have worked my ass off out there and this is what you do to me! . . . You keep me from supervising my workers— no wonder there are such delays. It will not be because of me that the war effort is jeopardized.[15]

Though his colleagues issued him a reprimand, they never bothered him in this way again.

He pretended to be angry with people when he really wasn't. He forced himself to display false bravado and would pace around before important meetings, getting his anger flowing and with it the need to be assertive in evil's face. He even made sure to wear clothing that authority above him respected, including high-topped black boots. He broke rules that others would be too timid and cowardly to breach. Courageous people follow the spirit of truth, which sometimes requires them to break law's letter and to defy unjust legislation, like Jesus and His disciples on the Sabbath, like Martin Luther King Jr. with segregation.

I want to return momentarily to Frank Peretti's testimony. Earlier you read how he was bullied, even tortured by fellow students. His ordeal did not get substantially better until a succession of pivotal events transpired.

Peretti made a sincere request to God after a bully sprayed deodorant in his eyes. He asked God to have mercy upon him and deliver him, to set him free from the torment. Then he went to gym class, a major stage for his humiliation, looking very ill. His dread got the better of him, and a teacher noticed . . . a teacher who then showed compassion. This small glimmer of light made Peretti feel hopeful, and he began to feel that fate might not always be against him. Encouraged, he wrote a letter to his appropriately named gym teacher, Mr. Sampson, in which he chronicled the abuse of the past several years.

His assertive approach paid off. Sampson sent him to the school counselor, who reviewed the letter and excused him from gym class for the rest of the school year. "We'll just call it a medical condition," he said.[16]

Frank Peretti's bullying nightmare received a substantial reprieve when a person in authority, who had the power to exert justice and the will to rescue, told a lie. Contrary to the counselor's claim, Peretti's body did not stop him from partaking in class. His assertion was completely false; both the counselor and Peretti knew it. The one helped extract the other from problems out of his control, a problem resulting not of his own actions but of unjust systems and practices.

Such actions are too common among the courageous to ignore. Jesus seems to endorse it when it's appropriate—see His parable of the dishonest manager (Luke 16, *The Message*). Acts of moral courage are sometimes committed through the conduit of dissimulation, the act of deliberately not telling the truth. For Frank Peretti, a lie was a key that turned the lock on his cell's door and began his long journey toward freedom and wholeness.

# HAVING WHAT IT TAKES

Fritz Graebe's courage also included the use of physical force. He once pulled an automatic weapon from his coat and made it clear he would shoot Ukrainian militiamen who were about to kill innocent and defenseless Jews.

> They seemed to understand the universal language of violence, but I was terribly frightened. I was certain I would be forced to fire the gun and people would be hurt. The Ukrainians had the same fear because they saw that mine was an automatic weapon and theirs were not.[17]

Justice Moshe Bejski of the Israeli Supreme Court, chairman of the Commission for the Designation of the Righteous, asked a question in 1974 that suggested an urgent new direction of inquiry by Holocaust survivors and, by extension, anyone who cares deeply about love, truth, justice, and righteousness: "Why was it that in approximately twenty states under Nazi occupation or influence, which had the combined population of hundreds of millions, there were relatively so few persons who were prepared to help those who were in such urgent need of relief during that period?"

Graebe was one of only a handful who possessed that strength of character. What made these precious few so courageous and heroic?

That's part of the question Perry London sought to answer in the early 1960s. He identified three significant shared characteristics in the rescuers:

(1) having a spirit of adventurousness
(2) identifying with a morally strong parent
(3) having the status of being socially marginal.

## HELPING KIDS EXPERIENCE ADVENTURE

(1) Get them into Scouts.

(2) Sign them up for church groups that do real adventure.

(3) Enroll them in sports, understanding the difference between recreational and competitive sports. If your child is not as skilled as his peers, the recreational level is usually the right choice. If he's skilled in a sport or is a quick learner and is motivated to get better, then the competitive level is a good choice.

(4) Send them to summer camp, and do not call them.

(5) Find out whether your local college or university offers classes on orienteering, the skill of finding your way through the outdoors.

(6) Have them ride along with a police officer.

## THE SPIRIT OF ADVENTURE

Graebe was adventurous. Remember how he taught himself to stop stuttering? He overcame intentionally, not rashly. Writes Huneke, "Graebe's spirit of adventurousness was humane, calculated, and purposeful."[18] This is part of the Greek understanding of *thumos,* the fighting spirit properly applied to life.

One of our greatest advocates for cultivating and rediscovering the spirit of adventure is John Eldredge, who writes,

Adventure is important for kids. It helps them test their mettle. But it needs to be the right kind of adventure.

Adventure with a purpose, in the service of something larger than their own desire to pump adrenaline and other chemicals through their veins that give them a legal high and nothing more. Expensive self-indulgence.[19]

An adventurous spirit helps us play our part in a world that contains real evil. Eldredge writes:

We live in a world at war. We are supposed to fight back. It is apparently a difficult reality to embrace, as witnessed by the passivity that marks much of modern Christianity. We just want the Christian life to be all about the sweet love of Jesus. But that is not what's going on here. You may not like the situation, but that only makes it unattractive—it does not make it untrue.[20]

God, Eldredge reminds us, is described as a warrior who leads armies (Exodus 15:3; Isaiah 42:13; Jeremiah 20:11; Psalm 24:7–8). *We are made in His image.* As to the familiar argument that Christians are not to resist evil—"That's God's job," many say—Eldredge reminds us of the following: "Resist the devil" (James 4:7) and "Resist him" (1 Peter 5:9).[21]

One obstacle to the adventurous spirit in kids is misguided discipline.

The church has largely presented discipline as "kill your heart and just do the right thing." That is terrible. It wearies the soul, and ends up destroying the heart—the very faculty you will need in the face of great trial and testing. Good discipline harnesses the passions, rather than killing them. When Jesus "set his face like flint" toward Jerusalem, he manifested an inner resolve that came from deep within, from his heart.[22]

Discipline is simply to keep our sin from destroying all the life God wants for us. Life is the point.[23]

The battle to behave yourself—the Christianity of "just don't do anything bad"—will not suffice, I assure you. Minding your manners needs no Warrior. The young man becoming a Warrior needs a bigger story.[24]

I once inherited a soccer player whom a previous coach didn't want because he "didn't behave himself." He had a reputation for being a hothead. I knew he had a temper, but it wasn't the flailing, incorrigibly feral kind. There was an intelligence to his passion that sometimes spilled into anger, but he wasn't an angry kid off the field. He wanted to do well and was frustrated when he didn't. He didn't like people taking cheap shots at him, either. He wasn't a passive participant in sport or in life.

I like players who have what I call "the jalapeño factor" in them. Though I was warned about this kid, that he might cost me a game by getting a red card or committing a major foul in the penalty box, he never did so in three full years. He never lost us a game. Instead, his passion, which I helped to channel, has helped us win many a contest. His teammates even voted him captain.

It's a tragic day when adults feel the need to kill a child's heart and passion. There's a sinister element to it. I think many adults try to drive passion out of a child's heart because it's disruptive to our comfortable and highly scripted lives. There's an unpredictability to the younger spirit that frightens us. It questions our assumptions and rationalizations. It refuses to conform, and my, how we love conformity. Their power isn't always offensive— rather, it strikes fear in us, which we find offensive.

I believe this is one reason people responded so powerfully to Jesus, some being attracted to Him and some being offended. This more powerful approach to life is part of the lighter burden Jesus tells us we receive when we follow Him. Though behaving more assertively takes more energy upfront, it requires far less energy in the long run. Assertive living is lighter, less encumbered living.

Kids need help figuring out where to put such prancing

energy, not how to kill it. They need help making it serve others and not just their own ambitions. It's a unique power that can help the timid and the weak.

One of the most deadly ways to kill the heart of a child, warns Eldredge, is through rigid moralism that doesn't include adventure and freedom. Countless Christian males, now adults, battle this pernicious spiritual ailment. They often don't see how it has ripped away adventure (and with it, courage) until they hit middle age. Their lives lack spark and wonder; they long to possess an animating spiritedness. They live mostly on life's sidelines—there's a core part of them that wants to get into the game but persistently refuses when faced with the fear. More than anything else, they need to know that *once they've gotten the boulder of courage to start rolling, everything gets increasingly easier with continued practice.*

## MORALLY STRONG PARENTING

Fritz Graebe's mother, his primary moral role model, provided him with consistent and unyielding views of right and wrong.

She both articulated and practiced her beliefs and values. She stressed qualities of constructive candor, honesty, empathy, insightfulness, and assertiveness; and she directed Fritz to make difficult decisions that would cause life to be better or easier for someone else.[25]

She was also a very religious person, having grown up in a Lutheran tradition. Because of certain incidents within her parish, however, she preferred not to associate with that institutional church. Her beliefs revolved around key Christian teachings.

- ▶ The Golden Rule: "Do to others what you would have them do to you" (Matthew 7:12).
- ▶ The parables of compassion, such as the Good Samaritan. (Luke 10:29–37)

► "Love your neighbor as yourself" (Matthew 22:39).[26]

She weaved these teachings into everyday conversations, explaining that they were the basis on which she performed acts of kindness. Graebe also noted that she "accepted people for their own worth, not because someone else told her about or spoke against them."[27] She was her own judge, which helped her avoid rumor, prejudice, and gossip.

## MARGINAL PEOPLE

Social marginality can include social class, political affiliation and viewpoint, economic status, religious beliefs and practices, education status, and so on. Fritz Graebe's stuttering certainly marginalized him—he felt the sting of being rejected and mocked by his peers. His family was poor but respected. His mother's German dialect was not common in their region. And the family's association with Jews before the Nazi campaign put them out of step with the anti-Semitic culture.

Graebe also held a disdain for seeking the approval of others. "My mother always urged me to do what I—I, not others— thought was best and right. I do not regret that I have followed this teaching . . . it has served me well."[28] Observes Huneke,

> Peer approval and the slavish accommodation of social conventions do not cause a person to spend four years risk-ing summary execution to save the lives of thousands of persons publicly branded as "parasites."[29]

# SEVEN ADDITIONAL TRAITS OF COURAGE

Huneke received two grants that helped him further research the makeup of rescuers and, in the process, help us delve deeper into the richness and mystery of what makes people courageous.

He found seven indispensable traits.

The first trait he discovered is *an empathetic imagination*. This means courageous people are able to place themselves in the shoes of another intensely and imaginatively.

The second trait is *a person's ability to present himself or herself as in control of a critical situation*. Sometimes this requires acting, as we see in Graebe's many acts of courage.

The third trait is *previewing for a purposeful life*. In order to be altruistic, a person must shun passivity and become proactive, pro-social. This approach is characterized by careful planning to act cooperatively and responsibly, anticipating opportunities for having a positive and beneficial impact in the lives or circumstances of others, and actively promoting the well-being of self and others. As if writing directly to parents, Huneke explains that these "skills to live a caring and helpful life are taught, learned, rehearsed, and practiced."[30] One of the most consistently alarming and regrettable conclusions of studies in "Samaritan behavior" demonstrates one of this book's major themes: People they tried to help have often been left at the mercy of their enemies because the rescuers failed to plan ahead. Their hearts were in the right place, but they lacked shrewd astuteness.

The fourth trait is *a significant personal experience with suffering or death* prior to the war. Graebe, as a young boy, watched wounded men return from World War I. And he witnessed people mistreating his brother due to his physical deformity.

> Fritz's sensitivity to and awareness of the suffering of others enhanced a caring attitude and encouraged his decision to be a rescuer. The suffering of another human being did not lead him to feel either revulsion or fear. It neither morbidly attracted him nor did it weaken his resolve to combat it.[31]

The fifth trait of all rescuers is *their ability to confront and manage their prejudices.* They "developed a certain worldview that enabled them to interpret the persecution of Jews and others as morally repugnant."[32] Graebe's association with Jews before the Nazi persecution helped him feel their full humanity. "The most salient idea to emerge from [a related] study is the fact that familiarity does not breed contempt. To the contrary, familiarity breeds acceptance and respect."[33]

The sixth trait is *the development of a community of compassion and support.* The majority of rescues were isolated, secret acts of kindness. Rescuers suffered tremendous amounts of fear, sometimes disabling fear. Many took weeks and months to regain courage for the next rescue. The most acclaimed communal rescues were orchestrated by religious-based groups with a long-term and carefully organized ethic that united the people. If they had worked alone, they would not have been able to rescue so many. Graebe carefully selected the most "courageous, intelligent, and compassionate people to serve with him in his secret and subversive operations."[34]

The seventh and final trait is *the ability to offer hospitality.* Most rescuers had an active role in a church at some point and were aware of the biblical texts on hospitable acts and lifestyle. Their most frequently quoted passage was that of the Good Samaritan, where Jesus tells us to identify with those who are imprisoned, naked, sick, hungry, thirsty, and foreign.

Hospitality is a powerful training ground for altruism, which must be present if one is to acquire courage. Said Henri Nouwen:

> In a world full of strangers, estranged from their own past, culture, and country, from their neighbors, friends, and family, from their deepest self and their God, we witness a painful search for a hospitable place where life can be lived without fear. . . . That is our vocation, to convert the hostis into a hospes, the enemy into a guest and to create the free and fearless place where brotherhood and sisterhood can be formed and fully expressed.[35]

TRAITS OF THE COURAGEOUS

Huneke ends his powerful work with the following summary that we must ponder as we aim to raise our children toward lives well-lived:

These common traits of the rescuers are skills that can be taught and learned. As people learn and practice them, others who are in distress are more likely to be the recipients of direct, meaningful intervention. *These skill-related traits do not develop out of nothing or come to a person accidentally. They must be rehearsed and affirmed in a way that ensures their continued refining and practice.*[36]

# Appendix
# SELF-TEST FOR PARENTS

*The following self-test is designed to help you ascertain where you and your child presently stand with fear, assertiveness, anxiety, courage, and so on. Evaluate the results for the purpose of beginning to make adjustments and changes as needed, starting with you and extending through your family. To the best of your ability, answer each question with one of the five options below.*

Scoring:
Always (4)
Usually (3)
Sometimes (2)
Rarely (1)
Never (0)

_____ Do you hear about a child abduction in another part of the country and then decide not to let your children out of your sight?

_____ Do you feel your children should not be responsible for household chores?

_____ Does your child have a bank account, and is he shown the value of compounding interest? Or if he's very young, does he receive an allowance, with guidance on how to spend it?

_____ Do you do your child's homework for her when she's stuck and struggling?

_____ Have you completed her larger school projects for her?

_____ Do you coach him from the sidelines during sports events (not simply lending a helpful word of encouragement, but constant instruction)?

_____ Do you lecture your child after games, pointing out each mistake?

_____ Is parenting for you a hassle with very few, if any, moments of play and joy?

_____ Do you refuse to let your kids out of your sight even when there's no danger present?

_____ Do you regularly intervene when your child is playing with another child?

_____ When someone gives instructive but painful-to-hear guidance about your child, do you end the friendship or snub the person later?

_____ Do you cut your child's meat or other food for him when he's old enough to do it himself?

_____ Do you attack coaches regarding your child's position or playing time instead of finding out how he needs to improve?

_____ Do you forbid your kids from getting really dirty?

_____ Are your children required to bow to all authority?

_____ Are your children expected to keep from making noise when inside the house?

_____ Do you teach your kids that Jesus was always kind and gentle?

_____ When a teacher tells you your child got into trouble in class, do you assume the teacher is wrong and your child is unfairly blamed?

_____ Do teachers avoid you when they see you in public?

_____ Is your child's favorite activity video games, watching TV, or shopping?

_____ When your child expresses negative emotions, do you move quickly to change his course and discourage his expression of them?

_____ When your child is playing with another child, do you tell her to "be nice" rather than "be good"?

_____ Is it intolerable for you that your child receive anything less than an A on a test or project?

_____ Do you stop your children from romping around outdoors because you fear they'll get hurt?

_____ Would you say that laughter with your child is rare in your home?

_____ When he's bullied, do you tell your child not to push back physically or verbally?

_____ TOTAL

**Results:**

80 to 104: Official Jellyfish, Chicken, and Wimp Factory. Change course immediately.

56 to 80: Still in Peril. Need continued alteration. Seek feedback.

32 to 56: Growing but Not Out of the Woods. Reevaluate what's best for your child.

8 to 32: On Track. Some room for improvement.

0 to 8: Kids on Target for Health, Wholeness, and Happiness!

# Endnotes

## CHAPTER 1

1. Aleksandr Solzhenitsyn, cited in Luci Shaw, *The Crime of Living Cautiously: Hearing God's Call to Adventure* (Downers Grove, IL: InterVarsity, 2005), 21.
2. Henri Nouwen, *The Genesee Diary*, cited in ibid., 29–30.
3. Hara Estroff Marano, "A Nation of Wimps" in *Psychology Today* (November–December 2004): 61.
4. Ibid.
5. *USA Today*, "Fear Is Shaping Our Children," posted 9/4/2006, by Patricia Pearson.
6. Ibid.
7. *www.psychologytoday.com/articles/index.php?term=pto-20041112 -000010&print=1.*
8. *http://www.usatoday.com/news/opinion/2006-09-04-fear-kids_x.htm.*
9. *www.time.com/time/archive/preview/0,10987,1202940,00.html* ("Does Fatherhood Make You Happy?").
10. Op. cit., @ *usatoday.com.*
11. George Barna, *Revolution* (Wheaton, IL: Tyndale, 2005), 14.

## CHAPTER 2

1. *http://music.aol.com/aiminterview/chat_kelly_clarkson.*
2. *http://www.psychologytoday.com/articles/index.php?term=pto-20041112 -000010&print=1.*
3. John McCain and Marshall Salter, *Why Courage Matters: The Way to a Braver Life* (New York: Random, 2004), 14.
4. Ibid., 15.
5. Ibid., 43–44.
6. In *Good Housekeeping* (June 2004): 121.
7. Ibid.
8. Ibid.
9. Ibid.

## CHAPTER 3

1. See Paul Coughlin, *No More Christian Nice Guy* (Minneapolis: Bethany House, 2005).
2. See Paul and Sandy Coughlin, *Married . . . But Not Engaged* (Minneapolis: Bethany House, 2006).
3. Hara Estroff Marano, *Why Doesn't Anybody Like Me?* (New York: Quill, William Morrow, 1998), 52.
4. Ibid., 196.
5. Dr. James Dobson, *The New Hide or Seek* (Grand Rapids: Revell, 1999), 140–41.
6. Marano, "A Nation of Wimps" in *Psychology Today*, 61.
7. Dr. Henry Cloud, *Integrity* (New York: HarperCollins, 2006), 159.
8. Ibid., 160, emphasis original.
9. *www.psychologytoday.com/articles/index.php?term=pto-20041112-000010&print=1.*
10. *The Sydney Morning Herald*, "Nice Kids, Shame About the Parents" (May 21, 2005).
11. *www.cbsnews.com/stories/2002/10/03/opinion/garver/printable 524246.shtml.*
12. *www.timesonline.co.uk/tol/news/uk/article614678.ece.*

## CHAPTER 4

1. Marano, "A Nation of Wimps," *www.psychologytoday.com/articles/index .php?term=pto–20041112–000010&print=1.*
2. Ibid.
3. Ibid., emphasis added.
4. Ibid.
5. See ibid.
6. Marano, *Why Doesn't Anybody Like Me,* 84.
7. Cited in ibid., 90.
8. Ibid., 180.
9. Ibid.
10. *www.washingtontimes.com/national/20070110-112456-1761r.htm.*
11. *http://reluctantentertainer.blogspot.com.*

## CHAPTER 5

1. Microsoft Encarta Online Encyclopedia 2006, *http://encarta.msn.com.* 1997–2006 Microsoft Corporation. All rights reserved.
2. Ibid.
3. *http://kimveer-gill-news.newslib.com/story/9375-18/*

4. U.S. Department of Health and Human Services, Administration on Children, Youth, and Families, Child Maltreatment 1997: *Reports from the States to the National Child Abuse and Neglect Data System* (Washington, DC: GPO, 1999). See: *www.acf.dhhs.gov/programs/cb/publications/ncands97/s7.htm.*

5. U.S. Department of Health and Human Services, National Center on Child Abuse and Neglect, *Third National Incidence Study of Child Abuse and Neglect: Final Report Appendices* (Washington, DC: US DHHS, 1997), A63–A64.

6. Warren Farrell, *Father and Child Reunion: How to Bring the Dads We Need to the Children We Love* (New York: Penguin Putnam Inc., 2001), 75–77.

7. Marano, *Why Doesn't Anybody Like Me,* 74.

## CHAPTER 6

1. Gavin De Becker, *Protecting the Gift* (New York: Dell, 2000), 67.
2. Safety Tips @ *www.amw.com/kids/kids_tips.html.*
3. De Becker, *Protecting the Gift,* 150.
4. Ibid., 152.
5. Ibid., 165.

## CHAPTER 7

1. *www.christianniceguy.com*
2. Lynne Hybels, *Nice Girls Don't Change the World* (Grand Rapids: Zondervan, 2005), 15.
3. Ibid., 12.
4. Ibid., 17.
5. Ibid., 23–24.
6. Ibid., 59.
7. Ibid., 62.
8. Ibid., 76–77.
9. Ibid., 90.
10. Dobson, *The New Hide or Seek,* n. p.
11. Ibid., 206.
12. Full article at *www.nacronline.com/dox/library/daler/theology.shtml.*
13. Quote from *Mere Christianity* in *A Year with C. S. Lewis: Daily Readings from His Classic Works* (San Francisco: HarperSanFrancisco, 2003).
14. Dobson, *The New Hide or Seek,* 15.
15. Ibid.

16. Kingdom Living, *www.dwillard.org/articles/artview.asp?artID=92*.
17. Cited in Mark Galli, *Jesus Mean and Wild: The Unexpected Love of an Untamable God* (Grand Rapids: Baker, 2006), 65.
18. From an interview the author had with Galli.
19. Ibid.
20. Ibid.
21. Ibid.
22. Ibid.
23. Ibid.

## CHAPTER 8

1. *http://www.cnn.com/US/9712/03/school.shooting.folo/index.html*.
2. *http://www.bullyonline.org/schoolbully/cases.htm*.
3. *www.thestar.com/printArticle/172190*.
4. Ibid.
5. Clyde Robinson, David Nelson, and Craig Hart, "Relational and Physical Aggression of Preschool-Age Children: Peer Status Linkages Across Informants" in *Early Education and Development* (16:2, April 2005).
6. Marano, *Why Doesn't Anybody Like Me*, 148.
7. *http://www.rowan.edu/news/display_article.cfm?ArticleID=1551*.
8. *http://www.iicyc.com/iicyc/news/articles/156*.
9. "Government publishes guidelines to tackle cyber-bullies @ iTnews .com.au."
10. *www.parade.com/articles/editions/2006/edition_04-092006/Tom_Cruise_cover*.
11. Bill O Reilly, *The O'Reilly Factor for Kids* (New York: Harper Paperbacks, 2005), 13–14.
12. *www.wsav.com/midatlantic/sav/news.printview.-content-articles-SAV-2006-08-31-0031.html*.
13. *http://www.bayofplentytimes.co.nz/storypring.cfm?storyID=3695673*.
14. *http://www.macclesfield-express.co.uk/news/s/215/215914_fairytale_ending_for_girl_who_defied_yobs.html*.
15. *http://www.dailyrecord.co.uk/news/tm_obejctid=17353110&method=full& siteid=66633&headling=cosmetic-surgery-on-nhs-for-kids-name_page.html*.
16. *http://www.signonsandiego.com/news/reports/younglives/20010514-9999_mzlcl5alaska.html*.
17. "School Shooters Tell Why" in *Chicago Sun-Times* Exclusive Report (October 15–16, 2000), 16.
18. *http://youthviolence.edschool.Virginia.adu/prevention/parnet-advice.htm*.
19. "School Shooters Tell Why," 3.

20. Ibid.
21. *http://www.secretservice.gov/ntac/chicago_sun/find15.htm.*
22. "School Shooters Tell Why," 10.
23. In ibid.
24. Ibid.
25. In *Good Housekeeping* (June 2004): 123.

## CHAPTER 9

1. Dr. Bill Maier, *Help! My Child Is Being Bullied* (Wheaton, IL: Tyndale House, 2006), 37. A Focus on the Family book. All rights reserved. Used by permission.
2. "School Shooters Tell Why," 9.
3. *http://youthviolence.edschool. Virginia.edu/violence-in-schools/survey-hoax.html.*
4. Marano, *Why Doesn't Anybody Like Me,* 86–87.
5. Ibid., 187.
6. Ibid., 140.
7. Cited in Maier, *Help! My Child Is Being Bullied,* 45.
8. In *The Weight of Glory,* emphasis added, n. p.

## CHAPTER 10

1. Dr. Martin Luther King Jr., from a sermon at Atlanta's Ebenezer Baptist Church.
2. Frank Peretti, *No More Bullies: For Those Who Wound or Are Wounded* (Nashville: W Publishing Group, 2003), 172.
3. Microsoft Encarta Online Encyclopedia 2006. h, 1997–2006, Microsoft Corporation. All rights reserved.
4. Ruth N. Koch and Kenneth C. Haugk, *Speaking the Truth in Love: How to Be an Assertive Christian* (St. Louis: Stephen Ministries, 1992), 199–200.
5. Sam Horn, *Take the Bully by the Horns* (New York: St. Martin's Griffin, 2003), 122–23.
6. *http://www.rzim.org/slice/slicetran.php?sliceid=1257.*
7. In Dr. Bill Maier, *Help! My Child Is Being Bullied* (Wheaton, IL: Tyndale House, 2006), 46–47, 61–62. A Focus on the Family book. All rights reserved. Used by permission.
8. Peretti, *No More Bullies: For Those Who Wound or Are Wounded,* 88, 90.
9. Frank Peretti, *No More Victims* (Nashville: Thomas Nelson, 2001), 14. Reprinted by permission of Thomas Nelson Inc.

10. Ibid., 22.
11. Ibid., 24.
12. Ibid., 25.
13. Ibid., 52.
14. Ibid., 27.
15. Ibid., 62.

## CHAPTER 11

1. Excerpt from James David Hunter, *The Death of Character: On the Moral Education of America's Children* (New York: Basic, 2001).
2. Christina Hoff Sommers, "Being a Man," review of Harvey C. Mansfield, *Manliness,* published in *The Weekly Standard* (April 10, 2006): 11:28.
3. Dobson, *The New Hide or Seek,* 159.
4. From a 1924 letter.
5. Cited in Charles Morris, LL.D., *The Lives of the Presidents and How They Reached the White House* (1903), n.p.
6. McCain and Salter, *Why Courage Matters,* 13–14. Used by permission of Random House, Inc.
7. Ibid., 200.
8. Ibid., 106.
9. Ibid., 198.
10. Ibid., 199.
11. Ibid., 86.
12. In John F. Kennedy, *Profiles in Courage* (New York: Harper Perennial Modern Classics, 2006), appendix, 25.
13. McCain and Salter, *Why Courage Matters,* 45–46.
14. Ibid., 86.
15. Ibid., 88.
16. Dr. Martin Luther King Jr., in one of his last sermons before he was assassinated.
17. McCain and Salter, *Why Courage Matters,* 50.
18. Ibid., 206.
19. Ibid.
20. Ibid., 113, 143.

## CHAPTER 12

1. Dr. Henry Cloud, *Integrity,* 31, emphasis original.
2. Ibid., 37, emphasis original.

Endnotes

3. Douglas Huneke, *The Moses of Rovno* (New York: Presidio Press, 1990), xiii.
4. Ibid., xii.
5. Ibid., xvii.
6. Ibid., 7.
7. Ibid., 13.
8. Ibid., 14.
9. Ibid.
10. Cited in Galli, *Jesus Mean and Wild*, 70.
11. Huneke, *The Moses of Rovno*, 24.
12. Ibid.
13. Ibid., 52.
14. Ibid., 36.
15. Ibid., 37.
16. Peretti, *No More Victims*, 46.
17. Huneke, *The Moses of Rovno*, 55–56.
18. Ibid., 179.
19. John Eldredge, *The Way of the Wild Heart: A Map for the Masculine Journey* (Nashville: Thomas Nelson, 2006), 97.
20. Ibid., 144.
21. Ibid.
22. Ibid., 150.
23. Ibid., 73.
24. Ibid., 167.
25. Huneke, *The Moses of Rovno*, 179.
26. Ibid.
27. Ibid.
28. Ibid., 180.
29. Ibid.
30. Ibid., 182.
31. Ibid., 183.
32. Ibid.
33. Ibid., 184.
34. Ibid., 185.
35. Henri J.M. Nouwen, *Reaching Out: Three Movements of the Spiritual Life* (New York: Doubleday, 1975), 46–47.
36. Huneke, *The Moses of Rovno*, 186–87, emphasis added.